Do the Poor Want to Work?

LEONARD GOODWIN

Do the Poor Want to Work?

*A Social-Psychological Study
of Work Orientations*

THE BROOKINGS INSTITUTION
Washington, D.C.

Copyright © 1972 by
THE BROOKINGS INSTITUTION
1775 Massachusetts Avenue, N.W., Washington, D.C. 20036

Library of Congress Cataloging in Publication Data:
Goodwin, Leonard
   Do the poor want to work?
   Includes bibliographical references.
   1. Work.   2. Poor—United States.   3. Work—
Psychological aspects.   1. Title.
HD4904.G65   301.5'5'0973   72-146
ISBN 0-8157-3205-8
ISBN 0-8157-3206-6 (pbk.)

3 4 5 6 7 8 9

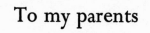
To my parents

THE BROOKINGS INSTITUTION is an independent organization devoted to nonpartisan research, education, and publication in economics, government, foreign policy, and the social sciences generally. Its principal purposes are to aid in the development of sound public policies and to promote public understanding of issues of national importance.

The Institution was founded on December 8, 1927, to merge the activities of the Institute for Government Research, founded in 1916, the Institute of Economics, founded in 1922, and the Robert Brookings Graduate School of Economics and Government, founded in 1924.

The general administration of the Institution is the responsibility of a Board of Trustees charged with maintaining the independence of the staff and fostering the most favorable conditions for creative research and education. The immediate direction of the policies, program, and staff of the Institution is vested in the President, assisted by an advisory committee of the officers and staff.

In publishing a study, the Institution presents it as a competent treatment of a subject worthy of public consideration. The interpretations and conclusions in such publications are those of the author or authors and do not necessarily reflect the views of the other staff members, officers, or trustees of the Brookings Institution.

Foreword

How POOR PEOPLE, especially black recipients of public welfare, feel about work is an issue surrounded by much opinion and emotion but little research. Current proposals for meeting the needs of the welfare poor have brought to the surface conflicting views about their work orientations. Do the poor really want to work, or do they reject this form of activity, preferring welfare or other ways of getting money? Social scientists have given this topic little attention until recently, so there is no established body of literature.

Understanding the differences and the fundamental similarities in the work orientations of poor and more affluent groups is the central concern of this study. Leonard Goodwin, a research associate in the Brookings Governmental Studies program, has developed a framework for understanding and measuring work orientations and how they relate to the work activity of the poor. Extensive efforts were made to gather data from a broad spectrum of poor and nonpoor people and to ensure the validity and reliability of responses. More than 4,000 persons were surveyed and the results checked for possible interviewer bias in responses. The traditional measures of statistical significance used in the text establish a basis for interpreting broad trends that appear in the data.

Mr. Goodwin argues that work orientations are both the influencers of current work activity and the results of past experiences. Differences between the work orientations of the poor and those of the nonpoor seem explainable by different environmental experiences. Living in poverty negatively affects a person's belief about his ability to achieve success, but does not appear to diminish life aspirations or the view that work contributes to self-respect.

An advisory committee composed of Edgar F. Borgatta of the University of Wisconsin, Elliot Liebow of the National Institute of Mental Health, and Lawrence Littig of Howard University made numerous helpful comments on the design of this study and on early versions of the manuscript. The comments of Gilbert Y. Steiner, Director of the Brookings Governmental Studies Program, of John Creager of the American Council on Education, and of several anonymous readers are also appreciated.

Reginald Monroe, Joseph Tu, and Helen Gordon Cook of the Social Science Computation Center at Brookings assisted in designing and using computer programs for analyzing the data in this study. Pauline Milius gathered follow-up data on former trainees in the Work Incentive Program from records in offices of the program. The study benefited greatly from the expert editing of Elizabeth H. Cross. The index was prepared by Lois Fern. Delores Burton patiently typed several versions of the manuscript.

The aid of the Manpower Administration of the U.S. Department of Labor in financing part of the research reported here is gratefully acknowledged. The Department of Labor, however, bears no responsibility for either the data or the views expressed. Nor do the author's views necessarily represent those of the trustees, officers, or other staff members of the Brookings Institution.

KERMIT GORDON
President

February 1972
Washington, D.C.

Contents

Text Tables

Text Figures

Appendix Tables

I

The Problem

ONE ISSUE on which public officials, scholars, and most other successful Americans agree is that employed work is a good thing.[1] They see it not only as providing money, but also as contributing to self-respect and status in society and adding meaning to life.[2] While employment has been relatively high during the past decade, there has been marked underemployment and unemployment of certain segments of the population, especially those located in the urban ghettos.[3] Continuing high underemployment rates in these concentrated areas and the increasing number of mothers with young children on welfare are matters of serious national concern.[4]

The federal government, as part of its effort to meet problems of poverty and underemployment, has initiated work-training programs on a nationwide scale. Efforts are being made to overhaul the social welfare system or to institute some form of guaranteed income. Clearly, however, work-training programs will be ineffective if poor people have little interest in working. And if they reject the importance of work, guaranteeing them an income might result in their leaving the work force. To design an adequate national policy for the employment of the poor, it is necessary to understand their views about life and work. But programs and proposals have been proceeding without this kind of knowledge. Is the underemployment of poor men the result of their not wanting to work, of their negative view of employment? Do poor mothers prefer welfare as a way of life to working to support their families? Are the children of welfare mothers growing up without any sense of the importance of work because they have neither father nor mother who is regularly employed?

Whether there is a great difference in the way various members of society view work is of interest to social scientists as well as to policymakers. The question has to do with the nature of stratification within American society. Some social scientists have claimed that the poor maintain a subculture significantly different from the culture of regularly employed middle-class persons—a "culture of poverty."[5] One could infer from this that the orientation toward work of the chronically poor contains negative elements and is unlike that of the nonpoor.[6]

Other investigators have held that any differences in orientation between the poor and the nonpoor are the result of the poor's adaptation to the situational facts of life and employment—that they do not reflect cultural differences.[7] Is American society stratified in such a way that the poor can be distinguished from the nonpoor by the way they view the important social activity of employed work? The culture of poverty thesis would receive support only if welfare recipients' views of work are shown to be markedly different from those of employed persons with incomes above the poverty level.

This book reports on a study of the work orientations of poor and more affluent people and attempts to discover whether the unemployed and underemployed have basically different orientations toward work than the regularly employed and persons whose parents have worked. The value of the findings depends on the meaning given to "work orientations" and how the latter are measured. An introduction to this task consists of reviewing previous findings about the poor's view of work, after which the concept of orientations is discussed.

Earlier Findings

Only recently have government agencies, businessmen, and social scientists become interested in the views of the poor, and there has been little research on the subject. This seems odd in light of the outpouring of studies on work attitudes.[8] They, however, are concerned primarily with regularly employed workers, and begin with the assumption that people want to work. A psychologist who is thoroughly familiar with research on work motivation remarked:

> As soon as we begin to ask ourselves serious questions concerning the *psychology* of poverty—what it is that the poor person thinks, feels, believes, desires—we are forced to fall back on the doubtful resources of speculation, guesswork, and remote inference. . . . Our knowledge concerning attitudes to work has largely been obtained through study of individuals for whom the sheer ability to work is not the major problem.[9]

For an unemployed population, special questions need to be asked; for instance, To what extent is work an important part of a poor person's life goals and self-identity? Lack of knowledge about this is not absolute. There have been a few highly informative participant-observation studies in which researchers have sought to understand the poor by sharing associations with them, and several surveys asking them about the desirability of work.

Participant-observation studies have the advantage of being able to report not only what people say but how they act in a variety of situations. A study of this kind was carried out in a housing project for low-income blacks in St. Louis. One of the researchers made efforts to help several men obtain jobs.[10] He discovered that they did not approach the job search eagerly and that, while they recognized the importance of work in providing money, they attached little self-importance to it. At the same time, when a group of men in this housing project were asked if the reason for their unemployment was that they simply did not want to work and preferred drinking, being with friends, or running around with women, less than one-third of them said yes.[11] Fewer than one-third of the married women interviewed thought that men were unemployed because they did not want to work.

The same paradox was found in a participant-observation study of some thirty underemployed black men in the District of Columbia.[12] For almost two years, the researcher visited and talked with these men, who were in their twenties and thirties, in the context of their daily activities. He too found that they attributed little self-importance to work, but he judged this to be the result of their having continually failed in the work world. Most were able to qualify only for unskilled, menial jobs. Even working full time, they could not earn enough to support a family. These men seemed to value work, but their inability to achieve success led them to seek self-fulfillment in other areas of activity and even, fearing failure, to refuse opportunities for better jobs.

The inference is that poor men probably do identify work with self-respect, but environmental circumstances stand in the way of their obtaining decent jobs, and they withdraw from extensive work activity. While this interpretation would be important for the design of public policy, it is based on very limited data. If a different street corner in a different city had been chosen, if a different housing project had been studied, would the results have been the same?

An in-depth study of white teen-age gangs in an eastern city indicates that certain of these youths basically scorn employed work.[13] Self-respect comes instead from skill at illegal activities. The St. Louis and District of Columbia studies do not indicate whether poor men place great positive value on illegal activities. Explicit comparisons of the views held about work and illegal activities within and among the various groups studied would be helpful, but they would be possible only if measures of specifically defined orientations had been made for each group. None of the participant-observation studies included such provisions—the data are qualitative rather than quantitative. Comparisons of any psychological orientations and their relation to actions, even between persons in the same group, are problematical without precise definition and measurement.

Another approach is the survey, which offers greater opportunity for gathering data from large numbers of representative groups of people and making quantitative comparisons among groups. There have been a few survey studies bearing on whether poor people want to work. The preference given work over other activities, such as being with one's friends, was measured for groups of male heads-of-household in California,[14] some of whom were receiving welfare payments. Results showed that the preference for work among black welfare recipients was approximately the same as that of the more affluent black and white men. Similar results were obtained in New Orleans. Poor blacks expressed as much willingness to make special efforts, such as moving from the city, to get better jobs as did the nonpoor blacks and whites.[15]

A survey of AFDC (Aid to Families with Dependent Children) mothers was carried out in New York City. One of the questions asked was, "Would you prefer to work for pay or stay at home?"[16] Seventy percent of the respondents said they would prefer to work. A similar question was asked in a nationwide study of women who were on or had applied for AFDC.[17] More than 80 percent of the welfare group said they would like to work if they could find a steady job.

Poor young people in the Job Corps gave great emphasis to education and hard work as the way to get ahead.[18] Their aspirations were for white-collar jobs and the material things of middle-class life. In a survey of a Puerto Rican area in New York City, carried out in conjunction with the Mobilization for Youth program,[19] questions about work were answered by both adolescents and adults of each household. Both agreed that hard work and ability were necessary for success. They wanted white-collar jobs for themselves or for their children. A survey connected with the Neighborhood Youth Corps was conducted in poor and in affluent districts of New York City.[20] One of the questions asked city participants as well as high school and college students in middle-class areas was, "Supposing that somebody just gave you the money you needed every week; would you like this better than working?" More than 72 percent of all groups responding said that they would rather be working. Hence, even slum youths expressed an interest in working that went beyond money as such.

The surveys indicate that the poor have a positive view of work. They deal, however, with only a few aspects of work, so the findings are limited. To ask merely whether a person prefers to work or stay at home ignores whether he believes that work contributes to self-development. The relation between wanting to work and beliefs about one's ability to succeed in the work world were not explored. Little attempt, moreover, was made to create scales with high reliability—scales that elicit consistent responses. Possible bias in responses—poor people expressing views they think interviewers want to hear rather than their actual views—was virtually ignored. Finally, none of these efforts were based on theoretical considerations leading to a deeper understanding of how psychological views about work relate to work activity.

These criticisms do not apply with the same force to all surveys. For instance, an attempt was made several years ago to use achievement-motivation theory and measurement to account for the job-hunting behavior of men who were out of work.[21] Applicants for job placement through their local employment service were interviewed. A portion of the interview consisted of responses to a projective test in which the interviewee was asked to tell stories about pictures of one or more persons involved in various situations. The responses were used to measure the general variable of achievement motivation: the interviewee's striving and competitiveness. The researchers claim some relation between the job-seeking behavior of respondents and measurements of their achievement motivation. But the small number of cases and the way results were analyzed make it doubtful that any significant relation exists. Such a generalized concept as "achievement-motivation" seems inadequate to illuminate the work orientations and work activity of the poor.

An attempt to make achievement-motivation theory more specific and applicable to the work activity of unemployed people was carried out in New Jersey a few years ago.[22] Six scaled variables, including "motivation to work" and "expectancy to work," were defined and measured. The several measures were then combined into a single measure of "behavior potential to work."

Considering a person's expectation about obtaining a job is a distinct advance, inasmuch as such expectation is likely to affect job-seeking activity. The major concept of "motivation to work," however, remains unclear. Among the items chosen to measure it are: "I think that working makes me feel that I am somebody important," and "I work because of the money." These represent quite different goals to be fulfilled through work. Why they were singled out as part of "motivation to work" is not clear.

In any case, little behavioral validity was found for the overall measure. The New Jersey questionnaire was answered by almost 500 persons in one of the federal manpower training programs who had sought work through their local employment service. The correlation between their "behavior potential to work" scores and behavioral criteria set by the researcher, such as the number of months employed during the previous four and a half years, was only 0.14. When these scales were used in a more recent study of poor persons, they showed essentially zero correlation with work performance.[23]

Another attempt to predict work performance from views about work was carried out with poor youths in a work-training program in Chicago.[24] Heavy emphasis was given to a measurement of personal efficacy: the extent to which a person believes that he, rather than external forces, controls his life. While this would seem important in predicting work activity, the correlation between the scores of eighty-seven program trainees on this variable and their postprogram earnings was virtually zero, which may be the result of the way the variable was measured rather than of a flaw in the general concept. Correlations of virtually zero were also found between post-program job earnings and scores on all the other psychological variables measured in the study, one of which was the "Protestant ethic."

This brief review emphasizes the scattered nature of research on poor people and work. Piecing together the information reveals that the surveys usually indicate that poor people believe in work, but the in-depth studies indicate that poor males neither look for work ea-

gerly nor believe it engenders self-importance. These divergent findings lead to the hypothesis that poor people lose interest in work
when they discover that their efforts do not lead to success. There are
too few data to permit the refinement of such a hypothesis or the
generation, much less the testing, of other hypotheses. Attempts to
show quantitative relations between views about work and work
performance have been largely unsuccessful. This failure may stem
in part from inadequately conceptualizing how the poor perceive the
environment. In particular, the attractiveness of income from sources
other than work—illegal activities and welfare payments—has not
been thoroughly explored. What seems to be called for in any case is
a more careful delineation and measurement of work orientations as
they relate to concrete activity in the work world.

The Meaning of Orientations

Work orientations are regarded in this study as psychological
attributes that significantly influence activity in the work world.
Hence, defining and measuring work orientations, and showing their
interrelations, are basic to understanding people's actions.[25]

There are, of course, other kinds of psychological factors—those
relating to personality, for example—that may influence work activity. Measurement of work orientations can provide at best an imperfect elucidation of the psychological influences on work activity. In
addition, conditions in the environment may be much more influential
than orientations. Certain persons, for instance, may have positive
orientations toward work but find no jobs open to them and hence
show no work activity. While orientations by themselves cannot
completely determine action, they can reveal the psychological potential for work, whether or not it is realized in face of resistances in
the nonpsychological environment. Thus normal expectations would
be of significant but not necessarily strong links between work orientations and work activity. Understanding the work orientations of
the poor might lead to realistic hypotheses (or policies) about the

changes in situational conditions necessary to change their work patterns.

Situational conditions, including social class status, provide the context in which psychological potential operates and at the same time significantly shape it. In the course of social experiences, which include family interactions, early schooling, and subsequent contact with the work world itself, people not only are guided by their work orientations but also undergo experiences that affect their orientations. That is, orientations are part of a feedback process in which the orientations influence action and then are themselves influenced by the action. The feedback sequence as it would operate over time is diagrammed in Figure 1-1.[26]

While our concern is with work orientations and work activity, the action model can be applied to other kinds of orientations and actions. An important point, which is not shown in the diagram, is that certain actions may have more influence on situational conditions than others.

FIGURE 1-1. *The Action Process*

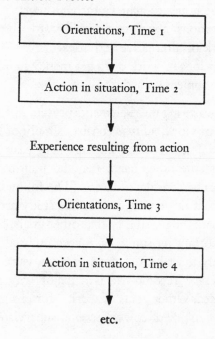

etc.

For example, a series of actions leading to high educational achievement in school may affect not only orientation toward education and work, but also the subsequent situation of being admitted to college. The final level of education reached in turn affects employability when entering the work force. So there is a complex and continuing interaction of orientations, actions, and changes in situations brought about by the actions. People experiencing different situational conditions can be expected to show certain differences in orientations. This study attempts to determine the differences and similarities in work orientations for the poor and the nonpoor.

This feedback concept of action becomes significant as the orientations, and the relationships among them, are made specific. The elements of orientations used in this study are taken from concepts that have been widely used by psychologists and sociologists.[27] Four elements that relate to work are the following:

Attitude—affective response to work, whether one likes it or dislikes it.

Goals—ends one hopes to achieve through work.

Beliefs—expectations about one's ability to obtain one's goals through work or alternative activities.

Intentions—decisions to work or to get money in other ways under various environmental conditions.

Defining and measuring these elements present differing problems. Since in the case of work, *attitude* consists simply of liking or disliking it, definition is clear-cut and measurement easy. Goals, beliefs, and intentions, on the other hand, may be multiple and complex. Which ones are to be considered basic? (The following discussion is meant to ensure that those measured in this study are important, but it does not eliminate the possibility that other goals, beliefs, or intentions, judged important by some, have been omitted.)

Money certainly must be included in any measure of occupational *goals*, since monetary recompense is a major way in which work activity is evaluated. Other goals of work—for example, a preferred kind of office or shop, or of coworkers and supervisors—fall outside the scope of this study. They refer to specific work conditions rather than to a general commitment to work activity. True enough, specific conditions encountered in the work situation may affect the general commitment. But it is the latter that is of concern here; it really centers on the extent of identification of self with work. It becomes important, then, to measure self-development as a goal of work—to learn the extent to which a person sees work as contributing to his self-respect. To know, too, whether work is related to other goals in life, such as good health and having a nice place to live, is especially useful in comparing responses of poor and nonpoor people. Does work occupy the same place in overall life goals for the poor as for the well-off?

Beliefs about the work context can also be multiple and complex. Take one example: the way to get a promotion is to always agree with your boss. But more basic than such job-related beliefs are those concerning one's ability to succeed in the work world. The action model developed here recognizes explicitly that environmental experiences affect people's psychology and are reflected in people's beliefs about the efficacy of their own efforts in achieving success in the world. How a man feels about his ability to succeed probably both reflects his past experiences and influences his working potential, and hence is an obvious candidate for measurement.

Intentions regarding work and other ways of obtaining money are many and intricate. This study examines particularly the acceptability of government support in the form of welfare and the willingness to engage in illegal activities—two forms of income maintenance that are the major alternatives for poor people if they do not work or do not earn enough by working. Also examined are the intention to get more training and education if poor, and the extent to which people say they would work even if they had an amount of money they thought sufficient.

Each of these four psychological elements is differently related to the external world. Intentions are the most closely tied to environmental conditions. Beliefs, while less constrained by reality, are still linked to certain kinds of situational outcomes, such as success in the work world. Goals and attitude are the elements least bound by external conditions. Whether one likes or dislikes work, or how much one identifies self-respect with work, may bear little relation to conditions in the work world.

Because of their conceptual differences, the elements would appear at first to be psychologically distinct. One might expect goals to be related to other goals but not to beliefs, for example. This is not the case, however. While a few orientations consist only of goal or intention elements, in others there is a clustering of goals with beliefs and of beliefs with intentions. None of the orientations, however, reveal a clustering of goals or attitude with intentions. Perhaps goals and attitude are not associated with intentions because the first two are the farthest of the four elements from concrete action, while the last is the nearest. As the mediating element between these two extremes, beliefs combine with either, but not both, in establishing orientations.

This study analyzes the nature of these orientations, how strongly they are held by the poor and the nonpoor, and how they are interrelated. The underlying assumption is that the statistical relationships among orientations correspond to psychological processes that guide people's actions. In later chapters the correlations between orientations and work activity (measured by the amount of money earned) will be examined and some hypotheses presented about the causal relations among the orientations and work. The action model will also be discussed in greater detail, and certain of its features tested.

2

Studying Work Orientations

THE PSYCHOLOGICAL ELEMENTS—goals, attitude, beliefs, and intentions—were measured by the work orientation questionnaire. It contains several sets of questions about work that are to be rated on four-step ladders, ranging, for example, from "Agree" at the top to "Disagree" at the bottom. Questions are also asked about age, education, and work experience. The questionnaire is reproduced in Appendix A. The substantive questions were selected after a pilot study (described in Appendix B) had been made which tested the feasibility of gathering this kind of information from the poor.

The items were further refined in the initial stages of this study. After 120 welfare recipients had completed the questionnaire, all the items measuring the elements were analyzed to determine if the respondents were clustering the items in the expected way. The technique of factor analysis was used in this clustering process.[1] A separate factor analysis was carried out on the items measuring each element to check the purity and reliability of that element. Similar analyses were made of small numbers of questionnaires answered by nonpoor groups to make sure that they were clustering items constituting the elements in the same way as the poor.

After more than 3,000 persons had answered the questionnaire, all the items measuring all the elements were clustered with each other, allowing the elements to combine into orientations. This was the initial step in the final formulation of the work orientations. Details of the analyses appear in Appendix B. The four ultimate criteria used to establish that a particular cluster of items was measuring a particular orientation adequately were: (1) the items were more highly correlated with each other than they were with items measuring other orientations; (2) they exhibited sufficient reliability or internal consistency to be useful in a research study (as shown in Appendix B, reliability coefficients for the orientations ranged from about 0.6 to 0.8); (3) they had a significant social-psychological interpretation; and (4) the content of the orientations for poor and nonpoor and for males and females was similar. (Elimination of a few items that were sensitive to the sex of the respondent led to orientations that were virtually identical for both sexes.)

Work Orientations

Presented below are nine clusters of items that define nine work orientations. The items constituting each orientation are labeled to make it apparent which elements have gone into it. A person's score on an orientation consists of the average of his scores on the individual items.

Orientation 1: Life Aspirations

This orientation, as shown in Table 2-1,* consists entirely of goal items—those appearing in the first section of the questionnaire. Life goals such as "having good health" are clustered with "having a nice place to live and plenty of food." But is only the obvious being measured? Who would not rate good health high? The significant issue, however, is that items about work—"having a regular job,"

* Tables measuring orientations appear at the end of this chapter, pp. 27–31.

"having a job that you like"—fall into this same cluster. Work activity is associated with other common life aspirations for the poor as well as the nonpoor. A person who scores high on the items measuring Orientation 1 is expressing high aspirations for certain aspects of his life, including work.

Orientation 2: The Work Ethic

This orientation (see Table 2-2) consists of the clustering of three elements: attitude toward work, self-development as an occupational goal, and the belief that one's efforts control success. Each of these elements emphasizes a different aspect of the involvement of the self in work. Together, they define what is commonly meant today by the work ethic. A person's liking for work is intimately related not only to his perception that work advances his self-development but to his belief that his own efforts lead to success. Those who score high on this orientation regard work as closely bound up with their own identity. The significance of this combination of elements is highlighted by the content of the next orientation.

Orientation 3: Lack of Confidence in Ability to Succeed in the Work World

Lack of confidence in one's ability to succeed at work, as reflected in this orientation, consists in part of a belief that external forces, such as "luck," control occupational success. Belief in fate might seem offhand to be the reverse of the notion that one's own efforts count most. In that case, one would expect the items measuring these two beliefs to have strong negative correlations and the items measuring external forces to cluster negatively in the work ethic orientation. That is, the work ethic would consist not only of positive endorsement of a person's own efforts yielding success, but also of an explicit rejection of external forces playing a major role in achieving success. This does not happen, implying that the two beliefs are not contradictory. The finding also suggests a flaw in the attempts by Rotter to measure in a single index belief in external versus internal sources of control over events.[2]

Items in this study that measure belief in external forces cluster with items that emphasize money as an occupational goal. Those who believe most strongly that success is a matter of luck or knowing the right people also hold money to be the most important reward of work. What social-psychological interpretation can be given to this compound of elements? People who have the greatest concern about money are likely to be people who have the least of it or who feel most threatened at the prospect of losing what they have. This is not to say that affluent people in secure jobs have no anxieties about money, but rather to suggest that after achieving a certain level of success in the work world people become concerned about other, nonmonetary goals; hence, monetary concerns decrease relative to all others. Put in terms of the questionnaire, high scores on the items emphasizing money as the most important reward of a job are likely to indicate lack of confidence about ability to earn sufficient money through work. This uncertainty about the effectiveness of effort is precisely what is measured by the items suggesting that external forces control success. It is reasonable to regard this orientation as measuring the respondent's lack of confidence in his ability to succeed in the work world. See Table 2-3 for a list of the questions for Orientation 3.

Orientation 4: Acceptability of Quasi-illegal Activities

Scores on this orientation measure the degree to which a person accepts quasi-illegal activities as a means of making money. The title of the orientation shows that the activities considered include ones that are explicitly against the law, such as peddling stolen goods, and ones that may not be, such as gambling.

As Table 2-4 shows, the first set of items in the orientation deals with assessment of these activities as ways of making a living. The second set concerns intentions. In this group, the last two questions ask for an opinion about what the respondent's best friend would do.

The rationale is that a person tends to project his own views onto a friend, and thus the responses here test those he gives about himself. The distinctive characteristic of these intention items is their specification of the context in which the proposed action would take place. Hustling or gambling is listed as an alternative to work when work does not yield enough to support a family. That respondents place desertion of their families under these conditions in the same category as marginal activities is some indication of the light in which they view them.

The other point to note about this orientation is that intentions combine with income beliefs but not with occupational goals.

Orientation 5: Acceptability of Welfare

Statements concerning the belief that government support is the best source of income constitute the first set of items in the welfare orientation. The second set involves intentions (attributed to the respondent himself and to a friend) to accept welfare in financial need. (See Table 2-5.)

Orientations 6, 7, and 9: Work beyond Need for Money, Train to Improve Earning Ability If Poor, and Work When on Welfare

These orientations are taken together as they consist of intention items only. Responses to them suggest what a person would do under three different kinds of economic circumstances. Orientation 6 concerns the intention to work even if the respondent had money he considered sufficient for his needs. Orientation 7 reverses the economic situation, and establishes whether the respondent, if he could not earn enough to support his family, would seek training or more education to improve his ability to earn. Orientation 9 measures women's intention to work if they are on welfare. (This applies only to women, since few men receive Aid to Families with Dependent Children.) The items are set out in Tables 2-6, 2-7, and 2-9.

Orientation 8: Job Discrimination

This orientation arises from responses to two statements (given in Table 2-8) about the role of racial discrimination in the failure of blacks to achieve success. The high correlation between the responses to these two items means that the measure formed by averaging the ratings is sufficiently reliable for the various groups in the study. If, as might be expected, blacks score much higher than whites on this orientation, the credibility—the unbiased character—of the responses will be substantiated.

The Respondents

More than 4,000 persons filled out the work orientation questionnaire. While budgetary limitations ruled out the possibility of collecting stratified random samples of the poor and nonpoor across the nation, it seemed likely that important information could be gathered from the responses of selected groups chosen to test suppositions about similarities or differences in work orientations.

1. To test the supposition mentioned earlier that receipt of welfare over a long period of time markedly affects the work orientations of mothers and their sons, interviews were carried out with a group of long-term AFDC (Aid to Families with Dependent Children) mothers and their teen-age sons. With the cooperation of the Baltimore Department of Welfare and based on the budget allocated for home interviews, a list of 356 black welfare mothers who had sons between the ages of fifteen and nineteen was compiled. The listing began with the mothers who had been on welfare the longest and continued through those who had come on welfare more recently.[3] Whites were not included because they constituted less than 5 percent of the longest-term welfare cases.[4]

Of the 356 families on the list, 267 mothers and their sons were interviewed in their homes.[5] There appeared to be no major differences in age, years on welfare, or number of children between those interviewed and those who could not be reached. The average length of time on welfare for the 267 families was sixteen years. Since the average age of the sons was seventeen, they had spent virtually their entire lives on welfare. Sidney Hollander Associates of Baltimore carried out all the interviews in that city, and recontacted 15 percent of the interviewees to check the validity of the interviews. The white interviewers were primarily middle-class housewives, as were the black female interviewers. The black male interviewers were made up of middle-class schoolteachers and lower-class young men. Differences in interviewer characteristics were used as checks on possible bias in response.

The welfare mothers and sons cannot in the technical sense be said to be representative of all long-term AFDC mothers and sons. On the other hand, there is no reason to believe that the work orientations of long-term recipients in Baltimore are much different from those of recipients in other industrial cities. There will be a chance, moreover, to compare their responses with those of a different group of welfare recipients (trainees in the Work Incentive Program) from various geographical regions and see if important differences are found.

2. To discover whether the length of time on welfare affects work orientations, short-term welfare mothers and sons in Baltimore were also interviewed. The names of 179 black mothers with teen-age sons were chosen from the list of AFDC welfare payees, but starting this time with the most recent case. (A recipient is issued a new welfare number only if she has no record of welfare assistance during the past five years. After five years' absence from the welfare rolls, a person's record folder and number is withdrawn.) Interviewed were 122 of these short-term mothers and sons, whose average length of time on welfare was one year.[6] The average age of the sons was seventeen.

3. An adequate interpretation of the work orientations of welfare mothers and sons also called for comparing them with the orientations of mothers and sons who are members of working families. Of particular interest were black families who had made it out of the ghetto —the formerly poor who had had some success in the work world. A

comparison would reveal the extent to which the work orientations of those who were successful differed from the orientations of those who had failed and remained on welfare.

There was no easy way to identify a group of black families who had been successful. It seemed likely that families leaving the ghetto would move to middle- or lower-middle-class areas of Baltimore that were undergoing racial change. Accordingly, census tracts were chosen that showed a marked increase in black population between 1960, when the census was taken, and 1967, when a market survey was done of the black population in Baltimore. An area probability sample of black families that included mother, father, and teen-age son or daughter was then drawn for home interviews. Details of the sample designation made by Sidney Hollander Associates, who also carried out these interviews, appear in Appendix B. In all, 500 black fathers, their wives, 250 male teen-agers, and 250 female teen-agers were interviewed. They are designated as outer-city black respondents. The interviewers for this group were black men and women of middle and low social status (high school graduates and high school dropouts).

4. As a further comparison with both the welfare and the outer-city black families, which would reveal whether marked differences in orientations were a function of race, responses were gathered from white families. To minimize differences in social-economic status, they were chosen from the same neighborhoods as the outer-city blacks. From the same census tracts showing racial turnover, an area probability sample of 175 white families—175 fathers, 175 mothers, 100 male teen-agers, and 75 female teen-agers—were interviewed by white middle-class men and women.

5. During the pilot study, a group of teen-agers from a small all-black, mostly poor community outside the District of Columbia, called Hickory Hill in this book, were interviewed. Further study of this group was undertaken because, as described in Appendix B, an earlier five-year participant-observation study of the community had been made. Results of this made it possible to identify all male teen-agers of a given age range about whom there was some independent

knowledge. Comparing the responses of this group with those of welfare sons could serve as a useful check on the validity of the latter's responses. Of the original group of 217 Hickory Hill youths, 168, who by now ranged from fifteen to twenty-one years of age, were interviewed; the rest could not be located, having left the area or gone into the Army. The interviewers were from Trans-Century Corporation of Washington, D.C.—two black men and two black women in their twenties who had some college background but were experienced in the street language and ways of poor blacks. Trans-Century made a 10 percent validation check of the interviews, and the signatures of respondents were checked against those obtained in the earlier participant-observation study.

6. All the groups mentioned so far come from the Baltimore–District of Columbia area. Responses to the work orientation questionnaire were also obtained at several other urban centers around the country from welfare recipients enrolled in a national work-training program called the Work Incentive Program (WIN).[7] The chief reason for including this group was that data could be gathered on work orientations during the initial period of participation in WIN, and that data subsequently related to trainees' work performance. (Trainees had been in WIN an average of two months when they completed the questionnaire.) Also, the orientations of these younger welfare recipients could be compared with those of the Baltimore recipients. A total of 1,439 WIN trainees completed the questionnaire in six cities: Baltimore and the District of Columbia in the East; Detroit and Milwaukee in the Midwest; the San Francisco Bay Area and Seattle in the West.[8] More than 80 percent were female, and of these 81 percent were black. Of the males, about 33 percent were black. The responses, technically speaking, are not representative of all WIN trainees in the country or of welfare recipients in general—they are probably typical of welfare recipients participating in training programs in nonsouthern cities. The results should therefore provide some basis for judging whether the orientations of welfare recipients vary by geographical region. The various groups responding to the work orientation questionnaire were:

Females

Long-term welfare mothers	267
Short-term welfare mothers	122
Outer-city black mothers	500
Outer-city black daughters	250
Outer-city white mothers	175
Outer-city white daughters	75
WIN trainees	1,185
Subtotal	*2,574*

Males

Long-term welfare sons	267
Short-term welfare sons	122
Outer-city black fathers	500
Outer-city black sons	250
Outer-city white fathers	175
Outer-city white sons	100
WIN trainees	254
Hickory Hill teen-agers	168
Subtotal	*1,836*
Total	4,410

That orientations with reasonable reliability can be established for different groups indicates that people responded to the questionnaire items in a systematic fashion. Further methodological issues were how to protect against systematic bias in responses and how to decide whether differences in ratings were really significant or simply the result of chance peculiarities in the groups studied.

Testing for Bias and Significance

It is necessary in any study to have some assurance that responses given to interviewers are reasonably accurate or unbiased. When responses deal with matters that can be checked against external criteria, direct measurement of bias is possible. When such measurement was made in an analysis of responses of black welfare mothers in New York City,[9] it was found that responses on such matters as voting registration and actual voting (as checked against records) were no more biased among welfare mothers than among other groups—both groups exhibited a tendency to overstate their voting activity. When it comes to factual information the problem of bias is no greater among the poor than among the more affluent. But what about responses to questions about opinion?

It is extremely difficult to check the bias of verbal responses, such as those to work orientation items, that have no concrete reference.[10] But assumptions about response bias, which lead to operational testing for such bias, are possible. The major assumption made here is that at the time of interview persons have a "true," or unbiased, response to the work orientation being measured; that is, both poor people and affluent people have a relatively fixed commitment to such issues as the work ethic. If a particular group has such a commitment and is answering in unbiased fashion, it should make no difference who is asking the questions—for example, a well-educated white woman or a black man with little education. The mean values of the group's ratings should be essentially the same. If, however, the ratings given to one set of interviewers are markedly different from those given to another set, the responses are assumed to be biased.

This argument is similar to one used in a study of response bias.[11] The researcher reasoned that, unless bias existed, equivalent groups of North Carolina blacks should give the same responses to black or white, high- or low-status interviewers. He found that there were marked differences in response ratings on questions concerning racial integration, a topic of considerable sensitivity. White interviewers and interviewers of higher social status than the respondents usually obtained more socially acceptable responses (against integration) than other interviewers. The conclusion drawn was that the race and social status of interviewers could decidedly bias the expressed opinions of black respondents. On this basis, it might have seemed advisable for this study to use only black interviewers of the same status as the respondents. It has been shown in another study, however, that for certain kinds of questions equality of status between interviewer and respondent introduces bias.[12] A similar finding is reported in the methodological study of New York City welfare recipient responses mentioned earlier.[13]

Previous research does not clearly indicate what combination of interviewer-respondent characteristics and item content lead to unbiased responses. Rather than make uncertain assumptions, it was decided to use interviewers of different class and race for this study, and to test for response bias. For example, equivalent subgroups of the 267 long-term and 122 short-term black welfare mothers who were participants in this study were interviewed by twenty persons. Of these twenty, eleven were middle class (at least high school graduates) and nine lower class (not high school graduates), thirteen were women and seven men. Three of the interviewers of long-term welfare mothers were white, but because it appeared that racial difference was biasing responses, the short-term welfare mothers were interviewed by blacks only. Correlations between interviewer characteristics and mean scores on the work orientations given by the 389 welfare mothers were calculated.[14] (The Pearson product-moment correlation coefficient is used throughout this book.) When a correlation of 0.20 or greater was obtained, bias was judged to be entering the responses; that is, respondents were considered to be rating items differently when interviewers had different characteristics.[15] It will be seen in the next chapter that no bias was observed in the mean values of five of the work orientations of long-term welfare mothers. Bias entered responses to the other four orientations.

A correlation greater than 0.20 was obtained, for example, between the scores of the black welfare mothers on the life aspirations orientation and the race of the interviewers. (This was the result entirely of long-term welfare mothers' responses because the short-term welfare mothers were interviewed only by other blacks.) The mean value given by the 89 long-term welfare mothers interviewed by the three white persons was 3.85, somewhat above the value of 3.66 given by the 178 mothers interviewed by the blacks. Which set of responses is "true" or unbiased? Since there is no external criterion against which to measure the "true" response, reasonable assumptions or procedures for decision making must be introduced. A fundamental concern in this study is to minimize the possibility of poor persons' giving work-oriented responses because they think the interviewer will thereby hold them in higher esteem. Whenever bias is suspected, the mean value that indicates lesser concern with work will be regarded as the less biased one. Hence, the lower mean value for Orientation 1, which measures life aspirations (including having a good job), is chosen as the less biased response of the black welfare women.[16]

When bias appears in ratings of certain orientations, such as job discrimination, it is not clear which rating is the less work-oriented one. Then the psychological meaning of the interviewee-interviewer interactions must be examined and the assumption made that respondents are giving ratings that tend to bolster their self-esteem.

The adjustments that have been made for interviewers' race, class, or sex are noted in the tables of the next chapters that present mean values and those that show correlations between work orientations. Certain interviewer characteristics are held constant (or controlled) in determining the correlation coefficients when such characteristics have an appreciable influence.

After examining responses for bias and making corrections where necessary, there still remains the task of determining whether differences between mean values are significant or can be attributed to chance variations in the several groups. A standard way of determining the significance of differences between two means is the t test, but traditional application of this test is not entirely appropriate for the purposes of this study. For one thing, it is based on the assumption that samples of respondents have been drawn at random, which is not true of respondents in this study. More limiting is the fact that differences between means may technically be statistically significant but of little practical import. Differences as small as 0.10 point on a four-step scale may be significant in a study of hundreds of respondents. This book is concerned with large differences and with major trends among poor and nonpoor groups.

At the same time the opposite peril of ignoring all differences between means because they do not seem large enough should be avoided. Some magnitude must be set as an approximate indicator of substantially different responses from two groups to the same work orientation. This is done by using the t test under the following circumstances. The smallest group analyzed in detail (100 outer-city white sons) and the largest standard deviation exhibited by that group on an orientation (0.94 for job discrimination) are chosen for the test. A value of 0.33 is thereby obtained as the difference between means which, in traditional phraseology, is statistically significant at the 0.01 level of probability.[17] This difference of 0.33 would be of even greater statistical significance for groups larger than 100 and orientations with smaller standard deviations. The magnitude of the difference, moreover, is greater than 10 percent of the total range of a four-point scale. Hence, a variation between means of 0.33 point can reasonably be taken to be substantial as well as statistically significant, and will be used as the indicator of substantial differences.

Since the scales in this study have limits (1 at the bottom and 4 at the top), the same difference in means that occurs near either extreme of a scale may reflect greater psychological difference in orientation than that which occurs near the middle. The risk here is that certain real differences in orientation at the extremes of the scale will be ignored because the 0.33 value is too large. Most mean differences observed in this study, however, are either substantially below or substantially above the indicator level. This level will not be applied mechanically; emphasis will be given to marked trends in the data and to consistent differences and similarities among groups.

Besides differences between means, subsequent chapters examine relations among orientations and between orientations and work performance. These relations are measured by the Pearson product-moment correlation coefficient. The standard statistical test for judging correlations to be different from zero, the t ratio, will be used. But again attention is focused on general patterns and trends among correlation coefficients rather than on statistical significance levels as such.

TABLE 2-1. *Work Orientation 1: Life Aspirations*

Questionnaire number	Item[a]	Psychological element[b]
6	Having a regular job	Life goal (job and money)
11	Having a job that is well-paid	Life goal (job and money)
21	Having plenty of money to get what you want	Life goal (job and money)
22	Having a job that you like	Life goal (job and money)
28	[Males only] Supporting a wife and family [Females only] Having a husband who supports you and your family	Life goal (job and money)
31	Having a nice place to live and plenty of food	Life goal (job and money)
35	Having a good education	Life goal (job and money)
7	Helping other people	Life goal (relations with others)
14	Getting along with your neighbors	Life goal (relations with others)
25	Getting along well with your family	Life goal (relations with others)
34	Making this a better world to live in	Life goal (relations with others)
10	Being honest	Life goal
19	Having good health	Life goal
26	Having important goals in life	Life goal

a. Items were rated on a four-step ladder, ranging from "Best way of life" at the top down to "Worst way of life."

b. The phrases in parentheses describe the clusters that emerged when the positive life goal items were factor-analyzed by themselves, rather than with all items together.

TABLE 2-2. *Work Orientation 2: The Work Ethic*

Questionnaire number	Item[a]	Psychological element
89	Most people like to work	Attitude
91	I like to work	Attitude
101	If I don't have a regular job, I don't feel right	Attitude
127	I feel good when I have a job	Attitude
85	Getting recognition for my own work is important to me	Occupational goal
86	Work should be the most important part of a person's life	Occupational goal
95	A man really can't think well of himself unless he has a job	Occupational goal
97	To me, it's important to have the kind of work that gives me a chance to develop my own special abilities	Occupational goal
105	Work is a good builder of character	Occupational goal
107	To me, gaining the increased respect of family and friends is one of the important rewards of getting ahead in an occupation	Occupational goal
115	Hard work makes you a better person	Occupational goal
121	To me, it's important in an occupation that a person be able to see the results of his own work	Occupational goal
113	Success in an occupation is mainly a matter of hard work	Occupational belief
122	Success in an occupation is mainly a matter of how much you know	Occupational belief
139	Success in an occupation is mainly a matter of how much effort you put into it	Occupational belief

a. Items were rated on a four-step ladder ranging from "Agree" to "Disagree."

TABLE 2-3. *Work Orientation 3: Lack of Confidence in Ability to Succeed in the Work World*

Questionnaire number	Item[a]	Psychological element
119	I like the kind of work you can forget about after the work day is over	Occupational goal
125	To be really successful in life, you have to care about making money	Occupational goal
129	To me, work is nothing more than a way of making a living	Occupational goal
132	The most important part of work is earning good money	Occupational goal
87	Success in an occupation is mainly a matter of knowing the right people	Occupational belief
99	Success in an occupation is mainly a matter of luck	Occupational belief
110	In order to get ahead in a job you need to have some lucky breaks	Occupational belief
126	In order to be successful in a job, people have to like you	Occupational belief

a. Items were rated on a four-step ladder that ran from "Agree" to "Disagree."

TABLE 2-4. *Work Orientation 4: Acceptability of Quasi-illegal Activities*

Questionnaire number	Item[a]	Psychological element
44	Gambling	Income belief
51	Running numbers	Income belief
54	Peddling stolen goods	Income belief
62	Being a successful shoplifter	Income belief
70	Leave your family?	Intention
72	Make money at hustling or gambling?	Intention
75	Leave (his/her) family?[b]	Intention
77	Make money at hustling or gambling?[b]	Intention

a. Income belief items were rated on a four-step ladder that ran from "Best way of getting enough to live on" to "Worst way of getting enough to live on." Intention items were rated on a four-step ladder from "Certainly would do that" to "Never would do that." These items were prefaced by the statement, "Suppose you could not earn enough money by working to support yourself or your family, using the ladder tell me how much you might do each of the following things."

b. This question was asked in the context of what the respondent believed his best friend would do.

TABLE 2-5. *Work Orientation 5: Acceptability of Welfare*

Questionnaire number	Item[a]	Psychological element
45	Being on welfare	Income belief
55	Having the government send you enough money every week	Income belief
58	Having the government give you a decent place to live and enough food and clothing	Income belief
68	Go on welfare?	Intention
73	Go on welfare?[b]	Intention

a. Income beliefs were rated on a four-step ladder that ran from "Best way of getting enough to live on" to "Worst way of getting enough to live on." Intention items were rated on a four-step ladder from "Certainly would do that" to "Never would do that." These items were prefaced by the statement, "Suppose you could not earn enough money by working to support yourself or your family, using the ladder tell me how much you might do each of the following things."

b. This question was asked in the context of what the respondent believed his best friend would do.

TABLE 2-6. *Work Orientation 6: Work beyond Need for Money*

Questionnaire number	Item[a]	Psychological element
64	Suppose you inherited enough money so that you and your family could live comfortably without your ever working, would you go ahead and work anyway?[b]	Intention
65	How do you think your best friend would answer that question—what number would (he/she) choose?	Intention
66	Suppose the government sent you as much money every week as you could get by working at a regular job. And suppose you could keep the government money even if you continued in in that job. Would you go ahead and work anyway?	Intention
67	How do you think your best friend would answer that question—what number would (he/she) choose?	Intention

a. Items were rated on a four-step ladder from "Certainly would do that" to "Never would do that."

b. This item was adapted from a Morse and Weiss study in which the item was to be answered yes or no, rather than rated on a scale; there was also an open-ended follow-up question as to why one would work or not work. See Nancy C. Morse and Robert S. Weiss, "The Function and Meaning of Work and the Job," *American Sociological Review*, Vol. 20 (February 1955), pp. 191–98.

TABLE 2-7. *Work Orientation 7: Train to Improve Earning Ability If Poor*

Questionnaire number	Item[a]	Psychological element
69	Get more education, if you were paid enough while learning?	Intention
71	Enter a job-training program, if you were paid enough while in training?	Intention
74	Get more education, if paid enough while learning?[b]	Intention
76	Enter a job-training program, if paid enough while in training?[b]	Intention

a. Items were rated on a four-step ladder that ran from "Certainly would do that" to "Never would do that." The items were prefaced by the statement, "Suppose you could not earn enough money by working to support yourself or your family, using the ladder tell me how much you might do each of the following things."
b. This question was asked in the context of what the respondent believed his best friend would do.

TABLE 2-8. *Work Orientation 8: Job Discrimination*

Questionnaire number	Item[a]	Psychological element
92	Racial discrimination is a major reason why Negroes don't get good jobs	Occupational belief
102	A Negro with a good education has much *less* chance of getting a good job than a white person with the same education	Occupational belief

a. Items were rated on a four-step ladder from "Agree" to "Disagree."

TABLE 2-9. *Work Orientation 9: Intention to Work If on Welfare*

Questionnaire number	Item[a]	Psychological element
78	Go to work if there was a good place to leave your children while you were away?	Intention
79	Go to work if you could keep everything you made up to $150 per month without losing welfare payments?	Intention
80	Go into a job-training program if your welfare allowance remained unchanged?	Intention
81	Go to work if the job was close to home?	Intention
82	Go to work if such jobs as house-cleaning or waiting on tables at a restaurant became available?	Intention

a. Items were rated on a four-step ladder from "Certainly would do that" to "Never would do that." The items were prefaced by the question, "If you were on welfare, how much might you do each of the following things?" The questions were asked of women only.

3

Work Orientations of
Welfare and Nonwelfare
Mothers

THE BASIC ISSUE of this chapter is whether women on welfare (Aid to Families with Dependent Children—AFDC) feel differently about work than women living outside the ghetto whose families are intact. Within that broad framework, women with teen-age sons who have been on welfare a long time will be compared with those who have been on it a short time, and both in turn with younger welfare women enrolled in a work-training program.

The black welfare mothers with teen-age sons were chosen, as described in the last chapter, from the AFDC list of the Baltimore Department of Welfare. The younger welfare mothers were enrolled in the Work Incentive Program (WIN) at six different locations around the country. Data from the black WIN women only are presented in this chapter; the smaller number of white women are mentioned in a later chapter. These WIN data from the different geographical regions are pooled because, as seen in the detailed presentation in Appendix C, regional differences are small.

Black and white women living outside the ghetto but still within the city limits of Baltimore were chosen on an area-probability basis. Each woman was part of a family unit that included a husband and a teen-age child.

Characteristics of the Study Groups

Table 3-1 reports the characteristics of the various groups of mothers. The average age of the welfare and outer-city mothers of both races

TABLE 3-1. *Characteristics of Welfare and Nonwelfare Mothers*[a]

Characteristic	Long-term welfare	Short-term welfare	WIN[b]	Outer-city black	Outer-city white
Age	43	41	29	41	45
Years of schooling	8	9	10	11	12
Number of children	3.9	...[c]	2.8	3.7	3.0
Years on welfare	16	1	3	...	...
Currently employed (percent)	*14*	*26*	...	*64*	*56*
Months on present job	15	9	...	35	23
Current weekly earnings (dollars)	52	54	...	78	68
Hours worked per week	29	30	...	34	26
Hourly rate (dollars)	1.80	1.80	...	2.30	2.60
Combined annual earnings of wife and husband (dollars)	2,800[d]	3,100[d]	...	9,100	11,200
Formerly employed, but now unemployed (percent)	*18*	*25*	...	*18*	*34*
Years at present address	...	...	...	5	12
Location of past address[e]	...	...	...	3.1	3.6
Number of respondents	267	122	957	500	175

a. All figures (except number of respondents) are averages.

b. The WIN respondents completed a self-administering form of the work orientation questionnaire, as described in note 8, Chapter 2. This form does not contain questions about current employment.

c. Estimated at about four.

d. Estimates based on an average monthly payment to each AFDC recipient in Maryland of almost $40 and the earned income reported by respondents in this study. For data on AFDC payments, see *Welfare in Review*, Vol. 7 (January–February 1969), p. 34.

e. Data gathered for outer-city Baltimore families only. The higher the number, the better the social-economic level of the neighborhood. Numbers 1 and 2 are in the ghetto; 3 and 4 are areas outside it. Present addresses for outer-city blacks and whites are almost uniformly 4. The percentage distribution of past addresses of these families is as follows:

	1–2	3	4
Black families	19	53	28
White families	9	25	65

was between forty-one and forty-five; the WIN mothers were ten
to fifteen years younger. The most noteworthy difference among the
groups, however, is in education. The long-term welfare mothers
at one end of the range have an average of eight years of schooling;
the outer-city whites, at the other extreme, averaged twelve years.
This variation is reflected in the income of the women who are working. The small percentage of employed welfare women earn only
$1.80 an hour, whereas the outer-city black mothers earn $2.30 an
hour and the whites $2.60.[1]

These data suggest that the black outer-city women would find it
hard to support their children without benefit of a husband's income.
Their prorated yearly income would be less than $5,000—hardly
sufficient to support the average of almost four children, especially
if day care were required for them. The black outer-city family units
are outside the ghetto primarily because both husband and wife bring
in income. Most of the outer-city mothers of both races either are
working now or have worked in the past.

Comparison of the Groups

On the basis of this information, certain speculations about the work
orientations of the various groups of women studied seem reasonable.
With their low level of education, their patchy work histories (only
about a third of the long-term and half of the short-term welfare
mothers had ever worked or were currently working), and their being on welfare, both groups of welfare mothers might be expected to
have little identification with work even while they show great concern about money. On the other hand, the WIN women, despite their
being on welfare, might, because they have entered a work-training
program, be expected to exhibit more positive orientations toward
work. Given their extensive work history and relatively good earnings, black outer-city mothers might be expected to show strong
work orientations, but their generally precarious economic and social
position would make signs of insecurity among them unsurprising. The
more secure economic position and better work record of outer-city

white women suggest that their interest in work would center less on the money it provides them than on its other, self-developing benefits.

Responses to Orientation 1

Table 3-2 presents the mean values given to each of the nine work orientations by the five groups of women. The first row gives the

TABLE 3-2. *Work Orientations of Welfare and Nonwelfare Mothers*
Mean values and standard deviations[a]

Orientation	Long-term welfare	Short-term welfare	WIN	Outer-city black	Outer-city white
1. Life aspirations	3.66[b] (0.32)	3.71 (0.34)	3.75 (0.34)	3.75 (0.23)	3.71 (0.24)
2. Work ethic	3.21[b,c] (0.52)	3.28[c] (0.45)	3.45 (0.39)	3.43 (0.36)	3.34 (0.36)
3. Lack of confidence in ability to succeed	3.13[d] (0.59)	3.13[d] (0.57)	2.77 (0.64)	3.19[e] (0.59)	2.61 (0.55)
4. Acceptability of quasi-illegal activities	1.26[e] (0.38)	1.16[e] (0.24)	1.17 (0.31)	1.12 (0.24)	1.04 (0.13)
5. Acceptability of welfare	2.92[d] (0.61)	2.88[d] (0.57)	2.31[d] (0.72)	2.12 (0.69)	1.53 (0.55)
6. Work beyond need for money	3.00 (0.84)	3.25 (0.81)	2.97 (0.81)	3.02 (0.92)	2.79 (0.91)
7. Train to improve earning ability if poor	3.69 (0.57)	3.71 (0.57)	3.73 (0.50)	3.63 (0.69)	3.62 (0.60)
8. Job discrimination	2.81 (1.14)	3.15 (1.04)	2.91 (0.99)	2.68[e] (1.13)	2.05[e] (0.91)
9. Intention to work if on welfare	3.23[e] (0.68)	3.15[e] (0.59)	...	3.42 (0.67)	3.43 (0.64)
Number	267	122	957[f]	500	175
Average age	43	41	29	41	45
Average years of schooling	8	9	10	11	12

a. All items making up each orientation were rated on four-point scales. The higher the rating, the more strongly the orientation is held. Standard deviations are shown in parentheses.

b. Adjusted for bias from interviewers' race.

c. Adjusted for bias from interviewers' class.

d. Ratings of welfare groups and the outer-city white group show substantial differences (at least 0.33 point).

e. Ratings of the black groups are substantially different from those of the white group.

f. Includes sixteen teen-agers with no children.

mean values for the orientation that measures commitment to various goals in life, called "life aspirations." Welfare mothers are found to have as high a life aspiration level as do outer-city mothers. The long-term welfare mothers give the lowest rating, 3.66, while the black outer-city and WIN mothers give the highest rating, 3.75. The difference between the two is only 0.09, far less than the 0.33 used as an indicator of a substantial difference between means. Emphasizing the insignificance of the difference is the fact that the 3.66 rating for long-term welfare mothers resulted after adjustment for bias arising from interviewers' race. (No adjustment appears for short-term welfare mothers because they were interviewed only by other blacks.) The adjustment was in the direction of a lower level of life aspirations.

INDIVIDUAL GOALS. While overall life aspiration level is the same for all five groups, it does not necessarily follow that the priorities given various goals are the same. To find out how much variation exists, the mean values of the ratings given seven of the fourteen goals constituting Orientation 1 are rank-ordered in Table 3-3. While ranking these ratings is risky because of the low reliability of single items, the focus will be only on differences that are large. To simplify the presentation, only seven goals were chosen (Appendix C contains the ranking of all fourteen). Six of the seven belong to a cluster called "job and money"; the other has to do with family matters and belongs to a cluster called "relations with others" (see Table 2-1). These clusters emerged when a separate factor analysis was made of the life goal ratings only.

The table reveals that welfare women are highly concerned about having a "nice place to live," ranking it near the top of the list (4, 2, and 3), a finding compatible with the speculation about welfare women's concern with money. Outer-city mothers, already living in fairly good conditions, place this goal near the bottom of the list (14 and 10).

Only white mothers rank the goal of having a *well-paid* job extremely low (12). The other four groups rank it higher, from 5 to 8, indicating that white mothers feel less need to make money. Having

TABLE 3-3. *Priority Given Certain Life Goals by Welfare and Nonwelfare Mothers*

Rank	Long-term welfare	Short-term welfare	WIN	Outer-city black	Outer-city white
1	...	...	Good education	...	...
2	Good education	Nice place to live	...	Good education	...
3	Husband supports you	...	Nice place to live	Husband supports you	Husband supports you
4	Nice place to live	Good education	...	...	Good education
5	Good family relations	Husband supports you	Like job	Well-paid job	Good family relations
6	Well-paid job	...	Well-paid job	...	...
6.5	...	Good family relations; Like job	...	...	...
7	...	...	...	Good family relations	...
8	...	Well-paid job	...	Like job	...
9	Like job	...	Good family relations	...	Like job
10	...	...	Husband supports you	Regular job	Nice place to live
11	...	...	Regular job	...	Regular job
12	...	...	...	...	Well-paid job
13	Regular job	...	...	...	...
14	...	Regular job	...	Nice place to live	...
Number of respondents	267	122	957	500	175

a *regular* job is placed near the bottom by long- and short-term welfare women; outer-city black and white mothers and WIN women give it somewhat higher rankings. None of them, however, give regular work a very high place in life's priorities.

All the women except those in WIN hold the goal of husband support much above the goals of regular or well-paid jobs for themselves. The WIN women, being relatively young and without an economically reliable husband, may have concluded that it is better to depend on oneself for support than on the kind of man they are likely to marry. However, even though they have enrolled in a work-training program, they give low priority to a regular job. This may indicate a certain ambivalence—while poor women recognize the importance of having a well-paid job, they are not convinced that being forced into the work world, with the responsibility of head of household, is a good idea.

OTHER RESPONSES. Respondents were asked to again use the four-step ladder on which they had rated life aspirations to indicate the extent to which they felt these goals had been achieved. (WIN trainees were not included.) As shown in Table 3-4, the women on welfare gave much lower ratings than the outer-city women. When asked why the rating was not higher, 40 percent of the welfare women cited lack of money or material things; only 21 percent of the outer-city mothers gave this reason. The responses are consistent with the much higher ranking welfare mothers gave to having a nice place to live.

Also cited by welfare women were family difficulties. Few outer-city women mentioned them; in fact, when asked why their life-rating was not lower, 19 percent of the white mothers spoke of positive aspects of family life. While 18 percent of the long-term welfare mothers also gave this response, only 10 percent of the short-term welfare mothers and 8 percent of the outer-city black mothers had anything positive to say. Thus family life seems to be rewarding to white outer-city mothers and to some long-term welfare mothers, but of less importance to the other two groups.

When asked, "What do you need to do in order to move up the

TABLE 3-4. *Life Fulfillment Ratings and Responses of Welfare and Nonwelfare Mothers to Open-ended Questions*

Item	Long-term welfare	Short-term welfare	Outer-city black	Outer-city white
Rating on four-step ladder	2.70	2.51	3.09	3.21
Question 39a: Why didn't you rate your present life higher?				
Answers (in percent)[a]				
Need more money; more food or clothing; better house; other	40	40	21	21
Trouble with children; not having husband; other	21	14	2	2
Not having a job; not having a good job	14	7	1	1
Question 39b: Why didn't you rate your present life lower?				
Answers (in percent)[b]				
Have some money; enough money; good house; other	30	30	46	72
Have a good family life; like my children; other	18	10	8	19
Question 39c: What do you need to do to move up the steps [of the ladder]?				
Answers (in percent)				
Get a job; get a better job	29	39	19	6
Get more money	40	40	32	28
Get more education or training	15	21	16	3
Number of respondents	267	122	500	175

a. Percentages based on respondents whose ladder rating was 1, 2, or 3.
b. Percentages based on respondents whose ladder rating was 2, 3, or 4.

steps [of the ladder]?" approximately one-third of the welfare women said, "Get a job," but only 6 percent of the outer-city white group gave that answer, apparently not perceiving their own work activity as a way of moving up in the world. Women on welfare, having no husbands to support them, see work-force participation as a way to alleviate poverty, but at the same time give much higher ranking to having a husband support them (Table 3-3).

Responses to Orientations 2 and 3

Orientation 2 measures the work ethic. High ratings indicate self-identification with work. No significant difference can be found among groups from the mean values given in Table 3-2, indicating that length of time on welfare is *not* associated with any loss in work ethic. This conclusion holds even for the long- and short-term welfare mothers interviewed by lower-class black male or female interviewers.[2] The earlier speculation that welfare women, having a sporadic record of work, would have little identification with work is not supported by the data.

This conclusion may seem at variance with traditional work-satisfaction studies, which indicate that lower-level workers are less interested in self-fulfillment through their work than are higher-level workers.[3] Most of these studies asked workers about their goals in relation to their current jobs. Reasonably enough, well-paid white-collar workers show more concern for self-development in their current jobs than do blue-collar workers. The questions asked in this study, however, bear on the goals that workers consider important irrespective of a particular job situation. Determining goals this way leads to similar results for different levels of workers or, as reported in Table 3-2, for recipients of welfare and nonrecipients.

One might still argue that the welfare mothers are merely parroting often-heard phrases about the work ethic that they do not really believe. There is no way to completely refute such an argument, because an absolute determination of what people "really" mean is not possible. But the relation of Orientation 3 to the work ethic should provide additional evidence of unbiased or valid response.

Orientation 3 measures lack of confidence in one's ability to succeed in the work world. The ratings in Table 3-2 reveal that white outer-city mothers have the lowest score (expressing greatest confidence) of any group. This is understandable in light of the economic success they and their husbands have achieved. Conversely, it is reasonable that the impoverished inner-city Baltimore mothers, who are not supported by husbands and whose own work efforts have not sufficed to keep them off welfare, should exhibit the least confidence. Also reasonable is the WIN mothers' rating between the two extremes. As welfare recipients, they have not been successful in the work world, but their participation in a work-training program suggests that they have more confidence in their ability to succeed than do other welfare recipients.[4]

But it is hard to understand the high rating of the black outer-city mothers.[5] Their economic position is less precarious than that of the welfare mothers, and their work efforts have brought some success. Their mean rating might thus be expected to fall between those of the welfare mothers and of the outer-city white mothers; instead, it is slightly higher than that of the welfare women. What makes these outer-city blacks so insecure? The reason may lie in part in their scantier education and lower family income as compared with the whites in their neighborhoods. Their race is also a factor, especially since 19 percent of them moved directly from a black ghetto to their present address (see Table 3-1, note e). Poverty and the ghetto are not nearly as distant psychologically or economically as they are for whites. An unforeseen setback beyond their control, such as severe illness or loss of a job, would readily expose these families to loss of the status they had achieved. Black women are insecure about their ability to move into a middle-class style of life for which they perhaps perceive their own and their husbands' preparation as inadequate. More generally, persons moving up who have to overcome environmental difficulties over which they have little control are probably very insecure.

Still another puzzle is presented by the correlations between lack of confidence and the work ethic. The expected correlation would be zero or negative. People who lack confidence in their ability should be neutral about or reject the work ethic with its emphasis on self-development and self-direction. In fact, however, the correlations shown in Table 3-5 are all positive.

This apparent contradiction of expectation will be considered first for the welfare mothers. All welfare women experience economic failure. All are poor and all must subsist on inadequate income provided by the government. The deeper the failure experienced, the less confidence one is likely to have in one's own abilities. For those

TABLE 3-5. *Correlations between Selected Work Orientations of Welfare and Nonwelfare Mothers*

	Orientation			
Orientation and group	2. Work ethic	3. Lack of confidence	4. Acceptability of quasi-illegal activities	5. Acceptability of welfare
1. Life aspirations				
Welfare mothers: Long-term	0.45[a]	0.14	−0.34[a]	0.08
Short-term	0.48[a]	0.17	−0.32[a]	0.10
WIN	0.18[a]	0.10[a]	−0.16[a]	0.02
Outer-city mothers: Black	0.25[a]	0.05	−0.21[a]	0.07
White	0.41[a]	0.17	−0.21[a]	0.09
2. Work ethic				
Welfare mothers: Long-term	...	0.26[a,b]	−0.23[a,c]	0.07[b]
Short-term	...	0.32[a,c]	−0.20[c]	0.00
WIN	...	0.22[a]	−0.11[a]	0.03
Outer-city mothers: Black	...	0.26[a]	−0.07	0.06
White	...	0.08	−0.20[a]	0.01
3. Lack of confidence				
Welfare mothers: Long-term	...	...	−0.06	0.23[a]
Short-term	...	...	−0.07[c]	0.05
WIN	...	...	0.08	0.31[a]
Outer-city mothers: Black	...	...	0.07	0.25[a]
White	...	...	−0.08	0.01
4. Acceptability of quasi-illegal activities				
Welfare mothers: Long-term	...	...	...	−0.01
Short-term	...	...	...	−0.05
WIN	...	...	...	0.09[a]
Outer-city mothers: Black	...	...	...	0.11[a]
White	...	...	...	0.15

a. Significantly different from zero at the 0.01 level of probability.
b. Adjusted for bias arising from interviewers' race.
c. Adjusted for bias arising from interviewers' class.

with the highest work ethic, the depth of their failure is measured not only by lack of money but also by inability to participate in the important self-developing activity of work. While they may blame their predicament less on themselves than on the inability of the fathers of their children to achieve job success and meet family responsibilities, they nevertheless live in a realm of "work failure," which lowers their feelings of self-worth. Women with a weak work ethic, on the other hand, do not expose their self-esteem to challenge in the work world and thus are less likely to lose confidence because of failure. This interplay would account for the positive correlations between Orientations 2 and 3.

The significant positive correlation exhibited by the black outer-city mothers is subject to the same interpretation. In their case, however, the crucial factor is the threat of failure rather than its actuality. In this group, mothers with the strongest work ethic risk not only economic failure in their effort to achieve middle-class status, but also damage to their identity. Mothers with the weakest work ethic risk less damage to their identity.

The very small correlation between work ethic and lack of confidence exhibited by the white mothers indicates that those of this group who identify with work are not particularly uncertain about their abilities. The finding is related to the more affluent and secure position of the group. Identification of self with work is not accompanied by a loss of confidence because success is already assured. It is also likely that the white mothers identify with their husbands' occupational success, which is much above that of the black husband, and do not risk failure through their own efforts.

These results suggest a new interpretation of the common finding that poor people strongly value "extrinsic" goals such as money, whereas affluent people emphasize self-development. The emphasis on money, as seen in several of the items that constitute Orientation 3, really indicates uncertainty about achieving success rather than denial of self-development or of the work ethic. Poor people's emphasis on money is positively related to self-development.[6]

The positive relation between work ethic and lack of confidence, together with the high mean values given the latter orientation by welfare women, is in sharp contrast to the response pattern of middle-class whites. This suggests that poor women are not mimicking middle-class responses, but are giving unbiased ratings that accurately reflect the realities of the poverty environment.

Responses to Orientations 4 and 5

The discussion thus far has focused on life aspirations, insecurity, and the work ethic. Next, alternative methods of income maintenance are considered.

All of the women strongly reject quasi-illegal activities.[7] According to the data in Table 3-2, poor mothers tend to accept such activities slightly more readily than do the more affluent mothers, but no group regards gambling and hustling as a preferred source of income.

Reasons for this rejection can be inferred from the pattern of correlations between scores on this and other orientations (see Table 3-5). If the negative correlations between quasi-illegal activities and life aspirations can be interpreted as corresponding to underlying psychological processes, all mothers appear to view participation in quasi-illegal activities as contrary to the good life defined by Orientation 1. The mothers also show a tendency, to judge from the negative correlations between work ethic and quasi-illegal activities, to see participation in these activities as a denial of the possibility of finding self-respect in work.

A clear-cut pattern emerges from the way the various groups rate the acceptability of welfare. As might be expected, the long- and short-term welfare mothers, who are most dependent on it, are the most accepting;[8] the white outer-city mothers are the least (see Table 3-2). Ranging between are the WIN mothers and the outer-city black mothers.

Within the welfare groups, the WIN women give the lowest rating to Orientation 5, as might be expected from their participation in an effort to get off welfare. But why do the short-term welfare recipients, who have been on welfare only one year, give such a high rating? In part, this may be because they are not typical short-term welfare recipients, who are young women with young children. The group in this study consists of women with teen-age sons, who have had to go on welfare at a time when their productive work years are waning. This undoubtedly leads to a strong feeling of dependence.

Ratings on this orientation provide a test of the validity of the responses to the questionnaire. Welfare clients would be most likely to slant their responses to items on government support toward middle-class acceptability. They must be aware that the middle class dislikes supporting welfare services, and would prefer to learn that the poor do not, in fact, want them. That the welfare mothers quite reasonably give higher ratings to this orientation than the more affluent women supports the belief that the poor are expressing their "real" views.

Further insights about acceptability of welfare are gained from the correlations reported in Table 3-5. None of the groups see welfare as a threat to life goals or as a rejection of the work ethic. Nor do they see any relation between welfare and quasi-illegal activities.

Positive correlations between the acceptability of welfare and lack of confidence are observed for the long-term welfare, WIN, and outer-city black mothers, who are probably trying to cope with their strong feelings of insecurity by finding welfare acceptable. Correlations of almost zero are shown by the short-term welfare mothers and the white mothers. In the case of the short-term welfare mothers, this is hard to understand. But a plausible explanation for the white mothers is that they have achieved such a high general level of security that even the least confident of them do not look toward government support to relieve that feeling. Further, the white mothers probably do not see themselves as the main supporters of their families. Hence, their feelings of insecurity in the work world are not directly translated into dependence on government support.

Responses to Orientations 6, 7, and 9

Orientation 6 concerns what people would do if they were well off; Orientations 7 and 9 their intentions if economically deprived. In the first case the items that make up the orientation seek to discover whether respondents would work even though they had enough money to sustain themselves and their families in a manner they thought adequate. In the second, the items reveal the tendency of respondents to further their education or training to improve their earning ability if they are poor; and in the third (which applies only to women), their tendency to work even though they are receiving welfare. Understandably, the ratings for all groups, taken together, are lower for Orientation 6 than for the other two—around 3.00 (see Table 3-2). There is one significant difference in ratings, which is not readily interpretable. The short-term welfare mothers seem much more willing to work if affluent than do the outer-city white mothers. One might expect the white mothers to give a high rating— they are the richest group and over half of them work. The short-term welfare mothers may feel that they can assert their independence most directly through holding a job. Twenty-six percent of them continue to work while on welfare, and a similar percentage worked previously, probably in an effort to stay off welfare (see Table 3-1). It appears in any case that women on welfare are no more inclined to leave the work force when they have "enough" than are the women who live more comfortably.[9]

There are no significant differences among groups in the intention to get training to improve their work skills. All groups of mothers give relatively high ratings (above 3.60), signifying that the women agree on the value of a better education or more training as a means of enabling them to support their families. (WIN women are of course acting on their expressed intentions.) They also agree that even if one is on welfare it is desirable to work. The average ratings for this orientation, however, run about 0.30 of a point lower than those for Orientation 7, because all women give a low rating, about 2.45, to the item in Orientation 9 that asks, Would you "go to work if such jobs as house-cleaning or waiting on tables at a restaurant became available"? Thus, while expressing a desire to work, none of the women care for menial jobs.

Though all the groups give about the same mean values to Orientations 7 and 9, they do not interpret these orientations in the same way, as the correlations in Table 3-6 indicate. For the welfare women, the degree to which they find welfare acceptable has no bearing on the strength of intentions to acquire more training or to work if they are on welfare. A closer relation (correlations of 0.14

TABLE 3-6. *Correlations between Selected Work Orientations of Welfare and Nonwelfare Mothers*

Orientation and group	Orientation		
	5. Accepta- bility of welfare	7. Train to improve earn- ing ability	9. Intention to work if on welfare
2. Work ethic			
Welfare mothers: Long-term	0.07[a]	0.34[a,b]	0.24[a,b]
Short-term	0.00	0.53[b]	0.48[b]
WIN	0.03	0.22[b]	...
Outer-city mothers: Black	0.06	0.06	0.10[b]
White	0.01	0.22[b]	0.22[b]
5. Acceptability of welfare			
Welfare mothers: Long term	...	0.07	0.07
Short-term	...	−0.01	−0.01
WIN	...	0.03	...
Outer-city mothers: Black	...	0.14[b]	0.21[b]
White	...	0.08	0.10
7. Train to improve earning ability			
Welfare mothers: Long-term	...	...	0.31[b]
Short-term	...	...	0.51[b]
WIN	...	...	...
Outer-city mothers: Black	...	...	0.27[b]
White	...	...	0.19[b]

a. Adjusted for bias arising from interviewers' race.
b. Significantly different from zero beyond the 0.01 level of probability.

and 0.21) appears for outer-city black mothers. This last group tends to read into the intention orientations an acceptability of welfare rather than the desirability of work *if* one is on welfare or the desirability of training *if* one cannot support one's family.

This same tendency is seen in the correlations with the work ethic. Outer-city black mothers see little relation between their identification with work and either training if poor or work if they are on welfare. Welfare mothers show a strong link between the work ethic and the intentions to get training and to work if on welfare, as, to a lesser extent, do the outer-city white mothers. The black outer-city mothers seem to be saying that being unable to support one's family or being on welfare precludes any contributory effects of training or work toward self-development. Such a viewpoint is not unreasonable for those who are outside the ghetto but are not yet entrenched in middle-class society. For the outer-city black mothers, finding themselves unable to support their families would be to dash all hopes for self-development. And obtaining training or work under those conditions (as projected in Orientations 7 and 9) would not contribute to their feeling of self-development.

Responses to Orientation 8

Further speculative insight into the psychology of outer-city blacks is gained by analyzing responses to the orientation concerning beliefs about job discrimination. This orientation consists of only two items, but they are so highly correlated as to yield a sufficiently reliable scale for measuring the extent of respondents' perception of racial job discrimination. The most obvious difference among the means in Table 3-2 is the extremely low value of 2.05 given by the white mothers, which indicates that they are aware of very little discrimination. Their rating may be justified by their residence in or near interracial neighborhoods, where they see that at least some blacks can afford houses like their own. They may also be aware that part of what passes for racial discrimination is really discrimination against the unskilled and uneducated. However, these white mothers, who do not personally experience racial discrimination, probably tend to underrate its existence.

The second noticeable feature of the means is that the short-term welfare mothers give this orientation the highest rating; next are the WIN mothers, then the long-term welfare mothers. Why this is so is not altogether clear. It may be that this sequence represents the extent of experience in the work force, although such an explanation would seem to be invalidated by the even lower rating of the work-experienced outer-city black mothers. They, however, are a special case; this is taken up in the next section. Whatever the reason, no interviewer bias is observed in the ratings of the welfare mothers.

The short-term welfare mothers, as noted earlier, were interviewed only by blacks, the long-term mothers by both blacks and whites. The latter tended to give white interviewers higher ratings on life aspirations. No such tendency appears in the job discrimination orientation. Long-term welfare mothers express the same views about job discrimination to white and black interviewers. This contrasts sharply with Thomas Pettigrew's report of several years ago that blacks respond differently when interviewed by different races.[10]

Bias among Outer-City Black Mothers

The bias detected in responses of the outer-city black mothers to the discrimination items is by far the most striking in the entire study. Lower-class interviewers (those who had not completed high school) carried out 217 interviews with outer-city black mothers. The mean value of the ratings given by these mothers to Orientation 8 was 2.14, while 283 outer-city black mothers gave an average of 3.22 to higher-class interviewers. The difference in means is 1.08 points! The correlation between the class status of interviewers and ratings on the orientation by all 500 mothers is a phenomenal 0.46.[11] These statistics probably indicate that the job discrimination items touch an issue outer-city blacks are very sensitive about—their status in society.

As noted earlier, outer-city black mothers have low confidence in their ability to achieve occupational success. Moreover, these families are economically insecure, depending in most cases on the income of both husband and wife and residing in or near neighborhoods where the income level of the whites is much higher.

If outer-city black families can be characterized as strongly upward-mobile and extremely self-conscious about their class status, they might want to impress a middle-class interviewer with their own accomplishments. The high rating on the job discrimination orientation would be a way of saying, "Yes, there is a great deal of discrimination in the job market, but because of my own superior abilities I have been able to overcome these difficulties and live in this nice neighborhood." It might also be a way of saying to one's socioeconomic peer, "I could have gone even higher than I have if it had not been for the discrimination that I met."

The outer-city black may not feel as threatened or as competitive in responding to the lower-class interviewer. Nevertheless, she may wish to assert her own superiority and higher status. Giving a low rating to the job discrimination orientation may be a way of saying to the lower-class interviewer, "No, there isn't much discrimination in the job market. The reason you haven't done as well as I is because you are really not as good as I am, or haven't worked as hard."

These interpretations are, of course, highly tentative. A great deal more data about the daily lives and feelings of the outer-city black families are needed to test them. That similar results are observed for the outer-city black fathers, and to some extent for the outer-city black sons, lends credence to the interpretations (see Chapters 4 and 5). The "true" rating of the black mothers on the discrimination orientation is difficult to determine. Responses given to both sets of interviewers may be "true" in the sense that this orientation varies with the context in which outer-city blacks find themselves. For present purposes the rating to be used for outer-city black women is the 2.68 average of the values given to the lower- and higher-class interviewers, but it is unrealistic to compare it with the means given by other black groups.

Two important ancillary points emerge from this case of response bias. The first is methodological: these findings would have gone unnoticed if interviewers of different class status had not been used. The second, of more substantive interest, is that the other orientations do not give rise to this kind of wide variability in response. It seems likely that it occurs only when the items touch on sensitive issues, such as status or identity, about which respondents are unsure or insecure. Additional research is required to explore this matter.

Summary of Findings and Conclusions

One inference to be drawn from the foregoing discussion is that the view of work held by any particular group is complex. To compare the views of different groups, the relationships among several work orientations must be examined. For example, all groups of women, ranging from long-term welfare to outer-city white, give equally high ratings to the work ethic (Orientation 2), but show a wide difference in beliefs about the effectiveness of their own efforts to achieve job success (Orientation 3). Long-term welfare women lack confidence in their ability while outer-city white women feel much more secure. Most striking, however, is the different relationship between these two orientations. The white outer-city women do not link them at all. The positive association of the work ethic with lack of confidence seems to characterize those who have failed, or are risking failure, in the work world.

All women rejected quasi-illegal activities as a source of income, regarding these activities as violations of their life goals. Welfare women find welfare much more acceptable than do the other women, and do not see such acceptance as violating their identification with work. All women seem willing to get further training and to work if they are on welfare or if they have "adequate" incomes, but the welfare women feel more strongly that such activities contribute to their self-development.

The findings that welfare women have a positive view of work but are insecure about their ability to achieve job success and dependent on government support when their own efforts fail cannot be attributed to long-term receipt of welfare as such. The WIN women have been on welfare only three years, and short-term welfare women only one year. The pattern of responses is probably typical of mothers in general who are poor, heads of households, and marginal to the work force.

The differences between welfare and outer-city mothers can be explained adequately on the basis of situational factors. A mother is understandably unsure of her ability to succeed and more willing to accept government support when she has an average of only about nine years of school and can earn little more than the minimum wage while having more than three children to support. The white outer-city mothers have ample reason to feel much more confident and to reject government help. They have twelve years of schooling, can earn considerably more than the minimum wage, and are members of families to which the husband contributes considerable income. *These findings do not support the position that there are cultural differences (differences in basic goals or values) between the poor and nonpoor with respect to work.*

The data on outer-city black mothers show that they are strongly committed to the work ethic, but uncertain of their abilities and highly sensitive about their class status. The findings are understandable in situational terms: though these mothers can earn much above the minimum wage, their total family income is substantially below that of white families living in similar neighborhoods, and descent into the ghetto remains a possibility.

Too often the task of helping persons move out of poverty is conceived wholly in economic terms. The responses from outer-city blacks suggest that there is a great deal of psychological stress associated with social mobility. Programs aimed at helping the poor should take into account that some persons are less able to withstand such stress than others.

Even while all the groups of women maintain the basic work ethic, responses to the life aspirations orientation suggest that they prefer a husband's support to having a regular, well-paid job themselves. This raises a question: Should welfare mothers be at home looking after their children or, because there is no working father, should they provide work models for their children? The next chapter examines the work orientations of the teen-age sons of four of the groups of mothers.

4

Work Orientations of
Welfare and Nonwelfare
Sons

This chapter considers whether teen-age boys brought up on welfare and without fathers lack interest in employment. Respondents are sons of the Baltimore long- and short-term welfare mothers and outer-city black and white mothers described in the previous chapter. A fifth group of teen-agers, between fifteen and nineteen, is from Hickory Hill, a small, mostly poor, all-black community just outside the District of Columbia (described in Chapter 2). Responses from this group are compared with the responses of the other poor teen-agers, but first certain background characteristics of the groups are examined.

Characteristics of the Respondents

Table 4-1 reports the characteristics of the five groups of youths, whose average age is seventeen. The educational level of the welfare youths is ninth grade; tenth grade for the outer-city black and Hick-

TABLE 4-1. *Characteristics of Welfare and Nonwelfare Teen-age Sons*[a]

Characteristic	Long-term welfare	Short-term welfare	Hickory Hill	Outer-city black	Outer-city white
Age	17	17	17	17	17
Years of schooling	9	9	10	10	11
School dropouts (percent)	17.7	19.0	17.3	10.5	3.0
High school graduates (percent)	7.5	5.8	11.3	8.9	28.9
Attending college (percent)	1.5	2.5	3.1	2.8	18.5
Years on welfare	16	1	...	...	...
Currently employed (percent)	33.7	19.7	43.7	32.0	51.5
Months on present job	5	4	6	6	6
Hours worked per week	26	24	29	25	21
Hourly rate (dollars)	1.80	1.80	1.90	2.00	1.80
Formerly employed, but now unemployed (percent)	28.2	11.6	13.7	21.5	19.0
Combined annual earnings of father and mother (dollars)	2,800[b]	3,100[b]	...	9,100	11,200
Number of children in family	3.9	...[c]	...	3.7	3.0
Years at present address	...	...	...	5	12
Number of respondents	267	122	128	250	100

a. All figures (with the exception of number of respondents) are averages.
b. Estimated. See Table 3-1, note d, for explanation.
c. Estimated at about four.

ory Hill youths, and eleventh grade for the white youths. These averages are affected by the dropout rate given in row three of the table: few of the white teen-agers have dropped out, but many welfare sons and Hickory Hill youths left school early, and very few are enrolled in college.

These data dramatize the limited educational background of the poor teen-agers. With the known relation of educational attainment to occupational status and income, many of them seem doomed to marginal positions in the world of work.[1] The kinds of jobs they now have, which pay about the minimum wage, probably are the same kinds they will qualify for as adults.

The situation of the Hickory Hill youths is slightly better. While their dropout rate is the same, a larger proportion graduate from high school. The situation of the whites, however, is quite different. While they earn little money now, their remaining in high school and going on to college will mean better-paying jobs later. The outer-city blacks are in an uncertain position. More of them than of the welfare sons stay in high school, but a 10 percent dropout rate is still substantial, and they are one year below their expected grade level. Some of them will probably complete enough education to get work that allows them to live at the same level as their parents, or at a higher one. Others may be unable to maintain that level.

Responses to the Questionnaire

Whatever the future holds for these youths, the question for this study is whether there are any differences in work orientations among them, and what effects parents have on their orientations.

Orientation 1 and Related Questions

Table 4-2 presents the mean values given eight work orientations by the five groups of youths. The first row gives the means for the orientation called life aspirations. All five groups show the same high level of aspirations. The priorities given the six positive life goals relating to job and money and the one goal bearing on family relations are presented in Table 4-3. The goal of having a "nice place to live" is ranked relatively high by the three poor groups, and relatively low by the outer-city blacks and whites.

The pattern of rankings given the life goal of "having a well-paid job" is much the same as that of the mothers in the last chapter: the white youths alone give it a low ranking (11); the others range from 2.0 to 5.5. The rationale for this pattern is the same. The white sons, living in more affluent circumstances, are less concerned about money; when they do earn, their contribution to the family income is a relatively small percentage of the total. The contribution of the welfare or outer-city black sons is much more important, so they rate having a well-paid job higher.

TABLE 4-2. *Work Orientations of Welfare and Nonwelfare Sons*
Mean values and standard deviations[a]

Orientation	Long-term welfare	Short-term welfare	Hickory Hill	Outer-city black	Outer-city white
1. Life aspirations	3.56[b] (0.44)	3.65 (0.38)	3.63 (0.26)	3.66 (0.29)	3.58 (0.27)
2. Work ethic	3.40[b] (0.42)	3.37 (0.44)	3.26 (0.41)	3.41 (0.35)	3.16 (0.43)
3. Lack of confidence in ability to succeed	2.99 (0.56)	3.12 (0.55)	3.19[c] (0.47)	3.14 (0.58)	2.49[d] (0.42)
4. Acceptability of quasi-illegal activities	1.35 (0.45)	1.27 (0.38)	1.55[c] (0.38)	1.26 (0.37)	1.26 (0.33)
5. Acceptability of welfare	2.38 (0.73)	2.44 (0.76)	1.83 (0.65)	1.97 (0.70)	1.69 (0.58)
6. Work beyond need for money	3.12 (0.82)	3.11 (0.86)	2.93 (0.70)	2.96 (0.91)	2.90 (0.70)
7. Train to improve earning ability if poor	3.72 (0.53)	3.70 (0.54)	3.62 (0.45)	3.71 (0.49)	3.50 (0.61)
8. Job discrimination	3.08[c] (1.10)	3.19[c] (1.05)	3.21[c] (0.94)	2.48[e,f] (1.11)	2.28[d] (0.94)
Number of respondents	267	122	128	250	100

a. Items were rated on four-point scales. The higher the rating, the stronger the orientation. Standard deviations are shown in parentheses.
b. Adjusted for bias from interviewers' race.
c. Adjusted for bias from interviewers' sex. Teen-age males are more likely to give unbiased responses to male interviewers than to female interviewers. The welfare teen-agers gave higher ratings to job discrimination (and Hickory Hill teen-agers, to lack of confidence and acceptability of quasi-illegal activities) to male interviewers.
d. Difference in means between either set of welfare sons and the white sons is at least 0.33.
e. Difference in means between either set of welfare sons and the outer-city black sons is at least 0.33.
f. Adjusted for bias from interviewers' class.

All groups give relatively low rankings to the goals of having a regular job and supporting a family. Since this probably reflects the youth of the respondents, one would expect quite different rankings from older males, such as the outer-city black and white fathers (see Chapter 5). High priority is given education by all the groups, even though about 18 percent of the poor youths have dropped out of school.

TABLE 4-3. *Priority Given Certain Life Goals by Welfare and Nonwelfare Sons*

Rank	Long-term welfare	Short-term welfare	Hickory Hill	Outer-city black	Outer-city white
1	...	...	Like job	Good education	...
1.5	...	Good education[a]	...	...	...
2	Well-paid job	...	...	...	...
3	Good education	...	Good education	Well-paid job	Good education
4	Nice place to live	Like job	Nice place to live	Good family relations	...
5	Like job	...	Well-paid job	Like job	...
5.5	...	Well-paid job; Nice place to live	...	...	...
6	Good family relations	...	Good family relations	...	Good family relations
7	...	Good family relations	...	...	Like job
8	...	...	...	...	Nice place to live
9	...	...	...	...	...
10	...	...	...	...	Support family
10.5	...	Regular job	...	...	...
11	...	...	...	...	Well-paid job
12	...	...	Support family	Regular job	Regular job
13	Regular job	...	Regular job	Nice place to live	...
14	Support family	Support family	...	Support family	:::
Number of respondents	267	122	128	250	100

a. This goal was given the same rank as another, not shown here. See Appendix Table c-1 for ranking of all the life goals.

When interpreting these rank-order results, remember that all the positive life goals are interrelated, that they all belong to the same cluster for both the poor and the nonpoor. That the poor groups show greater concern with material matters does not mean there is a fundamental difference in life aspirations for the poor and the nonpoor, but that the material aspect of life is more prominent for the poor within an overall orientation that is essentially the same for all.

This concern with material things is also seen in the poor sons' responses to other questions. As with their mothers, respondents were asked to use the four-step ladder to indicate the extent to which they felt their life aspirations were being fulfilled. They then were asked for reasons why their life-rating was not higher, or lower. As shown in Table 4-4, the poor sons, like their mothers, are more concerned about the need for money and a better house than are the sons living in more comfortable circumstances, who express satisfaction with those circumstances. The poor youths mention more frequently the need to obtain good jobs; and all groups see education as the best way of getting ahead in the world. Responses to these questions confirm the pattern observed in the rank-ordering of goals in Table 4-3.

The welfare sons' great concern about money, jobs, and education is accompanied by a strong awareness of not being able to satisfy these concerns, as seen by their relatively low life fulfillment ratings (see Table 4-4). Given their low educational level, lack of well-paid jobs, and low realization of goals, can these youths continue to maintain the work ethic?

Orientations 2 and 3

Table 4-2 shows no significant differences among the youths in the work ethic. In spite of wide educational, economic, and social differences, each group identifies with work to about the same degree, as do their mothers. The theory that sons who have spent virtually their whole life on welfare have lost the work ethic is not supported by the data.

TABLE 4-4. *Life Fulfillment Ratings and Responses of Welfare and Nonwelfare Sons to Open-ended Questions*

Item	Long-term welfare	Short-term welfare	Hickory Hill	Outer-city black	Outer-city white
Rating on four-step ladder	2.71	2.59	3.00	3.04	3.06
Question 39a: Why didn't you rate your present life higher?					
Answers (in percent)[a]					
Need more money, food, better house, other	29	20	20	10	14
Need better education	17	17	8	9	11
Poor family relations	4	5	2	1	4
Not having a job; need a better one	17	15	5	8	7
Question 39b: Why didn't you rate your present life lower?					
Answers (in percent)[b]					
Have some money	25	31	47	42	60
Have good family relations	17	5	5	9	20
Have a job	4	4	7	4	6
Have some education	15	10	5	6	15
Question 39c: What do you need to do to move up?					
Answers (in percent)					
Get more education or training	62	67	43	52	43
Get better job	43	44	20	33	22
Get more money	16	15	12	8	10
Number of respondents	267	122	128	250	100

a. Percentages based on respondents whose ladder rating was 1, 2, or 3.
b. Percentages based on respondents whose rating was 2, 3, or 4.

White sons give a significantly lower rating to the lack of confidence orientation than do the other groups, probably because they come from families of relatively high income and a long history of living in middle-class neighborhoods. As with the mothers, there are high levels of insecurity not only among the poor sons but among the outer-city blacks as well.

As shown in Table 4-5, positive correlations again appear between the work ethic and lack of confidence in ability to succeed for welfare and outer-city black sons. The explanation already given seems to apply here as well: persons who identify with work but have not achieved a high level of success in it tend to be insecure. The white

TABLE 4-5. *Correlations between Selected Work Orientations of Welfare and Nonwelfare Sons*

	Orientation			
Orientation and group	2. Work ethic	3. Lack of confidence	4. Acceptability of quasi-illegal activities	5. Acceptability of welfare
1. Life aspirations				
Welfare sons: Long-term	0.34[a,b]	0.16[a]	−0.36[a]	0.10
Short-term	0.44[a]	0.27[a]	−0.29[a]	−0.09
Hickory Hill youths	0.40[a]	0.02[c]	−0.23[a]	−0.06
Outer-city sons: Black	0.28[a]	−0.02	−0.23[a]	0.06
White	0.53[a]	0.06	−0.32[a]	−0.05
2. Work ethic				
Welfare sons: Long-term	...	0.17[a]	−0.42[a]	0.09[b]
Short-term	...	0.41[a]	−0.42[a]	0.31[a]
Hickory Hill youths	...	−0.01[c]	−0.39[a]	−0.11
Outer-city sons: Black	...	0.26[a,d]	−0.20[a]	0.06
White	...	0.29[a]	−0.30[a]	−0.13
3. Lack of confidence				
Welfare sons: Long-term	...	...	−0.05	0.29[a]
Short-term	...	...	−0.13	0.32[a]
Hickory Hill youths	...	...	0.23[a,c]	0.13
Outer-city sons: Black	...	...	0.07	0.18[a]
White	...	...	0.03	0.10
4. Acceptability of quasi-illegal activities				
Welfare sons: Long-term	...	...	...	−0.01
Short-term	...	...	...	−0.27[a]
Hickory Hill youths	...	...	...	0.39[a]
Outer-city sons: Black	...	...	...	0.13
White	...	...	...	0.20
7. Train to improve earning ability				
Welfare sons: Long-term	0.29[a]	...	...	...
Short-term	0.32[a]	...	...	...
Hickory Hill youths	0.37[a]	...	...	...
Outer-city sons: Black	0.15[a]	...	...	...
White	0.41[a]	...	...	...

a. Significantly different from zero at the 0.01 level of probability.
b. Corrected for bias arising from interviewers' race.
c. Corrected for bias arising from interviewers' sex.
d. Corrected for bias arising from interviewers' class.

outer-city sons, however, also show a positive correlation, whereas their mothers did not. This could be accounted for by the same dynamics, on the assumption that teen-age males in general are likely to be uncertain about their abilities, which have not yet been really tested. That there is no substantial correlation for the Hickory Hill youths remains a puzzle—one would expect them to follow the pattern of the other groups. Hickory Hill, however, is not typical of the urban ghetto though it is located close to one. The youths there are known to the other residents, are likely to spend most of their lives in the community, and identify with it. Thus, they may see the possibility of failure in the work world as less of a threat to their identity than do those in an urban ghetto.

Orientations 4 and 5

One might expect welfare youths to purposely lower their ratings on the items making up Orientation 4, which measures the acceptability of quasi-illegal activities, to avoid admitting to an interviewer any inclination toward socially unacceptable activities. Responses from the Hickory Hill youths are especially important in this connection because of all the poor groups, they should give the most unbiased and highest ratings. The Hickory Hill males were interviewed by two female and two male blacks who spoke the language of the streets. It was known from the earlier participant-observation study mentioned in Chapter 2 and Appendix B that extensive quasi-illegal activities occurred in Hickory Hill—various forms of hustling, gambling, and running numbers. The mean value given this orientation by young Hickory Hill males, as seen in Table 4-2, is higher than that of any other group. But the differences in means are not great, especially when the 1.35 of the long-term welfare sons is compared with the 1.55 for Hickory Hill. If the Hickory Hill responses are taken as valid, the ratings of the welfare sons are not abnormally low, not markedly biased toward middle-class standards.

Why does the Hickory Hill group give this relatively low rating to quasi-illegal activities? During the pilot study in Hickory Hill, open-ended questions were asked about ways of obtaining an income. One youth, who was known to participate in various forms of illegal activity, pointed out that he was never sure when or whether he would get his money, and that there was always the danger of being caught by the police. It may be that many low-income males who participate in illegal activities do not do so because they want to. Actions are guided not only by the psychological orientations measured in this study but by how persons view the situations in which they find themselves. A poor youth who cannot obtain money from his family or from a job may engage in petty theft, not because he really likes it, but because it is the only way he can think of to get enough money. The low mean values given this orientation make it quite conceivable that many poor youths would give up illegal activities if they could earn sufficient money at a job.

These data and arguments do not necessarily contradict Walter Miller's findings that members of certain groups like to engage in illegal activities and reject the importance of work.[2] It was found in the pilot study, for example, that the peer groups in Hickory Hill who were engaged in many illegal activities did reject the importance of work.[3] These groups, however, constitute only a minority of the Hickory Hill teen-agers. An overall view of all the teen-age males in Hickory Hill shows that most of them do not accept quasi-illegal activities as a desirable source of income. These findings warn against generalizing about the prevalence of certain orientations among the poor or in whole communities without making representative measurements. Results from Hickory Hill, it should be noted, cannot automatically be applied to the urban ghettos, since it is a small community with rural as well as urban characteristics and a stable population.

The mean ratings given to Orientation 5, the acceptability of welfare, as shown in Table 4-2, follow the same pattern as for the mothers. The welfare sons are much more acquiescent to this form of income maintenance than are the outer-city sons. The Hickory Hill youths, however, while poor, react more like the outer-city than the welfare males. How many of the Hickory Hill youths come from welfare families is not known, so it is impossible to tell whether their low rating reflects their not being dependent on welfare or a different view of it from that held in the Baltimore ghetto. But their view is different, as evidenced by the correlations between Orientations 4 and 5 shown in Table 4-5—like the outer-city whites, they see a positive relationship between the two. To them, accepting welfare is in the same category as engaging in an activity such as hustling. On the other hand, the welfare sons, like their mothers, clearly distinguish between the two ways of obtaining income.

The correlations of other orientations with 4 and 5 are also given in Table 4-5, and follow approximately the same pattern as that shown for the mothers in the last chapter. Quasi-illegal activities are seen as inimical to life aspirations and to the work ethic, while acceptability of welfare is seen as adverse to neither. The Hickory Hill youths show this same pattern.

Orientations 6 and 7

Orientation 6 measures the intention to work even if one has an adequate income. The mean ratings of all the groups are relatively high (they cluster around 3.00 and show no significant differences), suggesting an interest in work that transcends its monetary rewards.

Orientation 7 measures the extent to which a person would take training to earn more money if he were poor and could not support his family. All groups, including the welfare sons, strongly express this intention (see Table 4-2) and rate it higher than Orientation 6. This indicates, as it did for the mothers, that they are less interested in working if they have enough money than they are in improving their earning ability through training when they do not earn enough.

All groups strongly link Orientation 7 to the work ethic, Orientation 2, except the outer-city black sons, whose relatively low correlation of 0.15 suggests, as did their mothers', that there is such great concern about maintaining their somewhat shaky social status that training taken under conditions of not being able to support one's family could not contribute to fulfilling one's work ethic.

Orientation 8

Like their mothers, the outer-city black sons show a distinct bias arising from the class status of the interviewers. The value of 2.48 reported for this group represents the averaging of the 2.88 rating given to middle-class black interviewers and the 2.07 given to lower-class black interviewers. (The correlation between ratings and interviewers' class is again a very large figure, 0.37.) As in the case of the mothers, it may be that the sons are seeking to impress the middle-class interviewer by emphasizing that they and their families have "made it" even though there is much racial discrimination. And the low ratings given discrimination when the interviewer is lower class may be a way of telling him that he has failed to make it, not because there is discrimination, but because he has not tried as hard as the family he is interviewing.

Influence of Parents on Sons

One of the important issues to be explored in this study is the extent to which parents, especially welfare mothers, influence the work orientations of their sons. This influence is measured by the correlation between the ratings given on an orientation by each son and his mother.

A correlation coefficient does not in itself indicate either causality or the direction of psychological influence. It seems reasonable to assume that a mother's work orientation is firmly established before her son's; thus any influence would flow from mother to son. A significant correlation between the two sets of ratings would support the assumption that the mother has had some direct or indirect influence on her son's work orientation.[4]

The white outer-city mothers *and* fathers might be expected to have a greater influence on the work orientations of their sons than have the welfare mothers alone on those of their sons, especially in the case of Orientation 2, the work ethic. Surprisingly, Table 4-6

TABLE 4-6. *Correlations between Ratings of Parents and Those of Their Sons on Eight Work Orientations*[a]

Orientation	Long-term welfare	Short-term welfare	Outer-city black	Outer-city white
1. Life aspirations	0.39[b]	0.37[b]	0.13	0.05
			0.24[b]	0.07
			0.14	0.44[b]
2. Work ethic	0.35[b]	0.44[b]	0.30[b]	0.13
			0.38[b]	0.19
			0.33[b]	0.35[b]
3. Lack of confidence in ability to succeed	0.20[b]	0.43[b]	0.38[b]	0.12
			0.48[b]	0.19
			0.46[b]	0.42[b]
4. Acceptability of quasi-illegal activities	0.21[b]	0.40[b]	0.16[b]	0.09
			0.19[b]	0.09
			0.32[b]	0.02
5. Acceptability of welfare	0.25[b]	0.33[b]	0.29[b]	0.17
			0.36[b]	0.25
			0.48[b]	0.28[b]
6. Work beyond the need for money	0.21[b]	0.33[b]	0.10	0.05
			0.13	0.10
			0.14	0.01
7. Train to improve earning ability if poor	0.27[b]	0.42[b]	0.08	−0.07
			0.11	0.14
			0.25[b]	0.00
8. Job discrimination	0.26[b]	0.45[b]	0.36[b]	0.21
			0.41[b]	0.28
			0.34[b]	0.44[b]
Number[c]	267	122	250	100

a. The first row gives the correlation coefficient between the ratings of mothers and those of their sons; the second row gives the multiple correlation coefficient between the ratings of the sons and those of their mothers *and* fathers; the third row gives the correlation between the ratings of the mothers and those of the fathers of the same sons.

b. Significantly different from zero at the 0.01 level of probability.

c. "Number" refers to the number of respondents in each category being interrelated.

indicates just the opposite. The correlations between the white mothers and sons as well as between both white parents and their sons for the work ethic are insignificant. Correlations between the ratings of welfare mothers and sons are substantial, as are those between outer-city black parents and their sons.

The entire list of work orientations in Table 4-6 shows that the white mothers do not have a significant correlation with their sons for any orientation. Even when the influence of white fathers is added to that of the mothers, none of the multiple correlations reach significance. By contrast, both groups of welfare mothers and sons show significant correlations for all eight work orientations, and the black outer-city mothers, for four of them.

This pattern indicates that the white parents exert little influence on the work orientations of their sons,[5] an outcome that may seem so surprising as to throw doubt on the methods and groups used in the study. To provide more evidence of their validity, the correlations between the ratings of mothers and fathers are also presented in Table 4-6. Substantial husband-wife agreement for blacks as well as whites is seen on several important work orientations, such as the work ethic and job discrimination. The demonstration of such agreement through high correlations argues for the validity of the approach used, and therefore lends credence to the finding that white parents have little influence on the work orientations of their sons. (The low correlations might possibly be explained by very low standard deviations for white sons' and mothers' ratings, but Tables 3-2 and 4-2 show that the dispersion of scores is as great for whites as for blacks.)

This may mean that the white sons are gaining identification with work and strength in the other orientations outside the family: in schools, churches, and peer groups. It does not necessarily mean that white families have no influence on their sons' subsequent work activity. They are undoubtedly instrumental in their sons' adoption of the social manners and life styles conducive to obtaining and holding good jobs (welfare mothers may fare badly in this respect), but such variables were not measured in this study. Hence, the results offered here cannot be used to judge the overall contribution of family life to sons' future job attainment. But they do indicate clearly that, for the work ethic, welfare mothers have *no less* influence on their sons than do white parents in more affluent circumstances; indeed, they probably have a greater influence, encouraging their sons to identify with work.[6] Thus the theory that the welfare experience is depriving youths of the work ethic is not supported.

At the same time the significant mother-son correlations for the acceptability of welfare orientation and the relatively high mean values given it are evidence that welfare mothers are transmitting to their sons a greater tolerance of government support than is found among white outer-city families. To the extent that acceptability of welfare discourages work activity, one could argue that the mothers are transmitting a negative attitude about work. This also applies to the lack of confidence orientation, to which both groups of welfare mothers and sons give high ratings. The mother-son correlations are also significant, suggesting that mothers may be hindering their sons' entrance into the work force by transmitting their own uncertainty to them. It is of further interest to note the strong influence exerted by outer-city black parents on this orientation. The extent to which ratings on Orientations 3 and 5 actually hinder work activity is discussed in Chapter 7. What can be examined further at this point is whether the sons of welfare mothers who are working have different orientations than the sons of nonworking mothers.

Sons of Working Mothers

At the time welfare families were interviewed, in 1968 and 1969, the money earned by welfare women was deducted from their welfare payments. Hence, there was no monetary incentive for them to work. Nevertheless, 14 percent of the long-term welfare mothers and 26 percent of the short-term mothers were employed (see Table 3-1). Does having a working welfare parent favorably affect the work orientations of the son?

Table 4-7 presents the mean values given three important work orientations by the 67 welfare sons whose mothers work (sons of long- and short-term welfare mothers have been combined), and the 322 sons of nonworking mothers. All the sons are the same age and have had the same amount of schooling. No substantial differences for any orientation are observed. These data, limited though they are because of small numbers, give no support to the belief that the work activity of welfare mothers in itself vitally influences the work orientations of their sons.

TABLE 4-7. *Comparison of Mean Values Given to Selected Orientations by Sons of Working and Nonworking Welfare Mothers*

Work orientation or characteristic	Sons of working welfare mothers	Sons of nonworking welfare mothers
2. Work ethic	3.42	3.39[a]
3. Lack of confidence	2.92	3.05
5. Acceptability of welfare	2.25	2.43
Number of respondents	67	322
Age	17	17
Education (years)	9	9
Percentage employed	28	29

a. Adjusted for bias arising from interviewers' race.

Summary and Conclusions

The welfare and nonwelfare sons are more similar than dissimilar in their work orientations. Poor youths find quasi-illegal activities slightly more acceptable than do outer-city youths. The relatively low ratings given this activity by all groups, however, suggest that it is not a preferred means of income maintenance, and that many who participate in marginal enterprises would give them up if they could earn sufficient money in a job.

The most important conclusion to be drawn is that teen-age males who have spent virtually their entire lives on welfare have certain positive orientations toward work. Having no working parent in the home—neither mother nor father—has made the sons' identification with work no weaker than that of sons from families with working fathers.[7] This is not to say that lack of a working father has no effect on a household. A father undoubtedly influences the character of family life, but the influence can be negative as well as positive—it depends on how the father relates to other family members.[8] The point in any case is that welfare youths from fatherless homes show a strong work ethic, a willingness to take training, and an interest in working even if it is not a financial necessity. Their mothers favorably influence these positive orientations. The welfare experience has not destroyed the sons' positive orientations toward work.

However, two significant differences between black welfare and white nonwelfare sons should be recognized. Welfare sons are much less confident about their efforts leading to job success and much more willing to accept welfare if unable to earn enough money. There is evidence that welfare mothers directly influence the ratings of their sons, although the sons' ratings may also be explained by situational factors, such as their markedly lower educational level and family income. Thus if high ratings on these two orientations are shown to inhibit work activity, a more complex interpretation of the relation between work orientations and the effect of the welfare experience on formation of these orientations is necessary.

5

Work Orientations of Welfare and Nonwelfare Fathers

UNDER THE PROVISIONS of recent legislation, able-bodied fathers on welfare are required to participate in the Work Incentive Program (WIN). To determine the kind of work orientations held by poor men who have families and are receiving welfare payments, responses to the work orientation questionnaire were obtained from 244 WIN fathers at six sites around the country;[1] their race and region are shown in Table 5-1. To provide a basis for comparison, responses were also collected from 500 black and 175 white fathers living in the outer city of Baltimore. These men are heads of the

TABLE 5-1. *WIN Father Respondents, by Race and Geographical Region*

Region	Black	White	Total
East (Baltimore and District of Columbia)	19	2	21
Midwest (Detroit and Milwaukee)	22	37	59
West (Seattle and San Francisco Bay Area)	40	124	164
Number of respondents	81	163	244

family units whose wives and sons responded to the questionnaire, as reported in Chapters 3 and 4. With their continuous and successful participation in the world of work, they should exhibit orientations that are characteristic of the regular work force as a whole.

Characteristics of the Respondents

Table 5-2 presents certain characteristics of the welfare and nonwelfare fathers. The outer-city fathers are several years older than the WIN fathers, but the age difference should not affect the validity of the comparisons made between the two groups. The difference in

TABLE 5-2. *Characteristics of Welfare and Nonwelfare Fathers, by Race*[a]

	WIN fathers		Outer-city fathers	
Characteristic	Black	White	Black	White
Age	31	33	44	49
Years of education	10	9	10	13
Months on present job	...	...	58	58
Hours worked per week	...	...	38	42
Hourly rate (dollars)				
Present job	...	...	3.30	4.20
Previous job	2.40	2.60	...	...
Annual earnings (dollars)				
Present job	...	...	6,500[b]	9,200[b]
Previous job	4,600	5,000	...	...
Annual earnings of husband and wife (dollars)	...	...	9,100[b]	11,200[b]
Percent of total earned by wife	...	...	29	19
Number of children	3.5	3.7	3.7	3.0
Years on welfare	1.7	1.4	...	...
Number of weeks unemployed in year before entering WIN	34	32	...	...
Number of respondents	81	163	500	175

a. All figures (except number of respondents) are averages.

b. Only 93 percent of the black fathers and 97 percent of the white fathers were employed at time of interview. However, the average annual earnings are reported as if all were employed, because the unemployed fathers were receiving some form of pension or in a few cases unemployment compensation, and thus had job-related income. This should be counted to give a fair picture of family income, but the exact amounts were not determined in the interview. Hence, the earnings of those employed are used to estimate the annual earnings of all the fathers.

educational level is striking. White outer-city fathers have an average educational level of one year of college, whereas the black outer-city fathers average ten years of schooling. The educational level of the black WIN fathers and the black outer-city fathers is the same, but the white WIN fathers have the lowest level of all, nine years. In spite of this, the white WIN fathers earned more money than the black WIN fathers in their last jobs.

All WIN fathers earned enough money in their previous jobs to be above the poverty level (based on prorating their reported hourly wage). Their families probably had some feeling of economic achievement before difficulties put them on the welfare rolls.

The WIN fathers have families about the same size as those of the black outer-city fathers, but no direct information is available about their wives or children. Since the WIN fathers are younger than the outer-city men, their wives and children are presumably younger too. Having small children would decrease the work potential of these wives and thus the likelihood of their earning much, if any, income. The importance of this is shown by the figures in Table 5-2—outer-city black wives provide 29 percent of the family job income, while the white wives provide only 19 percent. The lower the family is on the economic scale, the more its economic viability seems to depend on the wife's contribution to the family income. Perhaps one of the reasons WIN fathers had to go on welfare was the inability of their wives to earn enough money.

Although WIN fathers have been forced to seek welfare, they are not long-term recipients. More than 75 percent of them have been on welfare one year or less. WIN fathers, furthermore, are not radically different, at least in the characteristics considered here, from outer-city black fathers who maintain economically viable families. WIN fathers earn slightly less, and so, probably, do their wives.

Responses to the Questionnaire

These differences in characteristics would not argue for drastic differences in work orientations between WIN and other fathers, although one might expect more insecurity and readier acceptance of government support among WIN males, especially the black ones.

Orientations 1 and 2

Table 5-3 shows no significant differences among groups in life aspirations. The WIN fathers have as great an interest in the "good life" as the outer-city fathers even though they are in difficult economic circumstances. Familiar differences appear in the ranking given certain of the life goals. Table 5-4 shows that the WIN males rate having a "nice place to live" fairly high, whereas the outer-city fathers, who already have nice places to live in, give it a low rank. The desire for a "well-paid job" is very low for the relatively affluent white fathers and higher for the other groups.

TABLE 5-3. *Work Orientations of Welfare and Nonwelfare Fathers*
Mean values and standard deviations[a]

Orientations	WIN fathers		Outer-city fathers	
	Black	White	Black	White
1. Life aspirations	3.61	3.63	3.71	3.66
	(0.63)	(0.48)	(0.26)	(0.27)
2. Work ethic	3.40	3.36	3.53	3.41
	(0.46)	(0.52)	(0.33)	(0.34)
3. Lack of confidence in ability to succeed	2.76	2.55	3.22[b,c]	2.44[c]
	(0.66)	(0.55)	(0.56)	(0.46)
4. Acceptability of quasi-illegal activities	1.33	1.32	1.34	1.15
	(0.52)	(0.49)	(0.31)	(0.28)
5. Acceptability of welfare	2.40	2.21	1.97[c]	1.61[c]
	(0.64)	(0.74)	(0.66)	(0.59)
6. Work beyond need for money	2.97	3.04	3.26	3.09
	(0.79)	(0.47)	(0.82)	(0.83)
7. Train to improve earning ability if poor	3.74	3.58	3.60	3.63
	(0.54)	(0.63)	(0.72)	(0.49)
8. Job discrimination	2.84	2.52	2.72[b,c]	2.15[c]
	(0.97)	(1.00)	(1.19)	(0.86)
Number of respondents	81	163	500	175

a. Items were rated on four-point scales. The higher the rating, the stronger the orientation. Standard deviations are shown in parentheses.

b. Adjusted for bias from interviewers' class.

c. Difference in means between outer-city white and outer-city black fathers is at least 0.33.

TABLE 5-4. *Priority Given Certain Life Goals by Welfare and Nonwelfare Fathers*

Rank	WIN fathers[a]	Outer-city black fathers	Outer-city white fathers
1	...	...	...
2	Good education	Well-paid job	Good family relations
3	Like job	Support family	...
4	...	Good family relations	Support family
4.5	Good family relations[b]	...	...
5	...	Good education	Like job
6	Nice place to live	Regular job	Regular job
7	Well-paid job	Like job	Good education
8	Support family	...	...
9	...	...	...
10	...	...	...
11	...	...	Well-paid job
12	Regular job	...	Nice place to live
13	...	...	...
14	...	Nice place to live	...
Number of respondents	244	500	175

a. Black and white WIN fathers have been combined to get a larger number for interpreting the rank ordering of individual items (as distinct from average scores of several items on a scale).

b. This goal was given the same rank as another, not shown here. See Appendix Table c-1 for ranking of all the life goals.

A "regular job" and "supporting a family" are ranked surprisingly low by the WIN fathers, while "good education" is unusually high. Poor men apparently put self-advancement ahead of family relations and support, with regular employment seen as least desirable. If this pattern indicates that WIN males have little interest in work, they should show a very low rating on Orientation 2.

Orientations 2 and 3

Table 5-3, however, shows that black and white WIN fathers rate the work ethic as high as the working fathers. This argues for a new interpretation of the life goal pattern. The low rankings given to a regular job and family support may be a symptom of the futility these men feel in trying to support a large family through the kinds of jobs with which they are familiar. The high rank given to getting a good education and the continued commitment to the work ethic probably indicate a desire to stay in the work force but to obtain higher positions through better education.

Since WIN fathers have failed to support their families through their own efforts, one would expect them to be less confident about their abilities than the outer-city fathers. And indeed, the expectation is borne out for the black WIN fathers when their rating is compared with that for the outer-city whites. The black WIN fathers also show less confidence than their white WIN counterparts, probably indicating that poor whites have been doing somewhat better in the work world and hence are less insecure than poor blacks. It is the outer-city black fathers, however, who show the greatest lack of confidence. These findings for the black fathers parallel those for the mothers and sons. High scores on Orientation 3 probably reflect the outer-city black father's feeling that illness, economic recession, or some other event beyond his control could lead to loss of income and downward mobility.

A surprise in the data is that welfare status makes no difference to the feelings of security the white men have. Failure in the work world apparently has not seriously shaken the belief of white WIN fathers in the effectiveness of their own efforts. Furthermore, as Table 5-5 indicates, the correlation between work ethic and insecurity for them parallels that of outer-city whites rather than that of their black WIN counterparts. It is essentially zero for both white groups, and significantly positive for both black groups. In the rationale for high or low correlations between these orientations developed in earlier chapters, it was argued that a positive correlation occurs among those who have failed, or who deeply fear failure, in the work world. Those identifying most closely with work undergo the greatest loss of self-worth from occupational failure and hence develop the greatest lack of confidence in their abilities. Among the occupationally successful, high identification of self with work does not carry with it

TABLE 5-5. *Correlations between Selected Work Orientations of Welfare and Nonwelfare Fathers*

	Orientation			
Orientation and group	2. Work ethic	3. Lack of confidence	4. Acceptability of quasi-illegal activities	5. Acceptability of welfare
1. Life aspirations				
WIN fathers: Black	0.29[a]	−0.02	−0.68[a]	−0.01
White	0.39[a]	0.00	−0.43[a]	−0.06
Outer-city fathers: Black	0.31[a]	0.09	−0.07	0.01
White	0.46[a]	0.24[a]	−0.09	−0.04
2. Work ethic				
WIN fathers: Black	...	0.25[a]	−0.34[a]	0.14
White	...	0.12	−0.39[a]	−0.15
Outer-city fathers: Black	...	0.33[a]	−0.01	0.03
White	...	0.16	−0.15	−0.08
3. Lack of confidence				
WIN fathers: Black	...	...	0.10	0.32[a]
White	...	...	0.24[a]	0.38[a]
Outer-city fathers: Black	...	...	0.16[a,b]	0.27[a]
White	...	...	0.10	0.23[a]
4. Acceptability of quasi-illegal activities				
WIN fathers: Black	...	...	...	0.22
White	...	...	...	0.22[a]
Outer-city fathers: Black	...	...	...	0.08
White	...	...	...	0.25[a]
7. Train to improve earning ability				
WIN fathers: Black	0.48[a]	...	...	...
White	0.33[a]	...	...	...
Outer-city fathers: Black	0.07	...	...	...
White	0.24[a]	...	...	...

a. Significantly different from zero at the 0.01 level of probability.
b. Adjusted for bias arising from interviewers' class.

the threat of insecurity about one's own abilities, and hence essentially zero correlations are observed.

This rationale explains the responses of the black WIN fathers, as well as those of the outer-city black fathers, in terms of their failure in the work world. The great insecurity of these fathers, like that of their wives and sons, can be attributed to a fear of failure to achieve middle-class status. But does this rationale adequately explain the responses of the white WIN fathers?

Inasmuch as the white WIN fathers have been unable to maintain their families without assistance, one might expect them to be like their black counterparts rather than like the outer-city whites. However, the average white WIN father had been earning an income above the poverty level and above that of his black counterpart about a year before. As far as can be ascertained from the current data, these white fathers have no history of indigence. They might, moreover, attribute their descent into welfare to an illness or a recession, events that do not basically challenge the effectiveness of their own efforts to succeed. In any case, a marked decrease in confidence may not occur immediately after the loss of a job. The insecurity of black WIN fathers probably arises not from the current welfare experience as such but from the continuing failure to earn as much as white men at the same educational level, and from a lifetime of discrimination and low standards of living within a ghetto. The argument, in short, is that one's view about the effectiveness of one's own efforts is not shaped by one or two events but evolves from one's life as a whole. The experiences of urban white men who are temporarily on welfare, it is suggested, do not stimulate as great a feeling of insecurity as the experiences of poor black men.

Several further points must be made. If this argument is valid, one would expect the same pattern of work orientations for long-term white welfare recipients as for black recipients, because these whites over time would have become more insecure about their abilities. Unfortunately, this hypothesis cannot be tested with the present data.

Another possibility is that the empirical data from the WIN men do not capture the characteristics of black and white welfare fathers, or perhaps they have some bias that is unique. However, if the WIN mothers (discussed in the next chapter) show the same pattern in comparative black-white responses as the WIN men, the validity of and explanation for the men's responses will receive support.

Orientations 4 and 5

Even if the orientation of whites toward the effectiveness of their own efforts is not changed immediately by the receipt of welfare, their orientation toward government support should change as a result of that experience. Both black and white WIN fathers appear to find welfare more acceptable than does either set of outer-city fathers (see Table 5-3). The trend in the mean values is quite pronounced. The fathers who are receiving welfare and are in greatest need of it in terms of their job-income capability—namely, the black WIN fathers—exhibit the highest acceptance of welfare. The white WIN males give the next highest rating, followed by the black outer-city fathers. The white outer-city fathers, who have the least need for government support, give by far the lowest rating. This sequence of mean values seems to follow economic rather than racial lines.

When the correlations between Orientations 4 and 5 are considered, however, there tends to be consistency along racial lines. The ratings given acceptability of welfare and quasi-illegal activities by the whites and the black WIN fathers show significant positive correlations. On the other hand, black WIN fathers and black outer-city fathers distinguish between income from welfare and from quasi-illegal activities, as indicated by correlations not significantly different from zero (see Table 5-5). The explanation for the positive correlations is not immediately obvious. They might occur because many fathers rate both orientations high or because they rate both low. Which of these conditions contributes most to the correlation can be determined only by examining the joint distribution of responses. Table 5-6 shows that only 19 percent of the white WIN fathers rate quasi-illegal activities *and* welfare dependence above the respective means for their group, while 33 percent of them rate both ways of obtaining income below their group average. The positive correlation between the two variables thus comes from the relatively low rating given to both. The same general conclusion holds for the outer-city white fathers, who tend to identify welfare income with income from such activities as "hustling," and to reject both strongly.

TABLE 5-6. *Percentage of White Fathers Giving High or Low Ratings to Both Acceptability of Quasi-illegal Activities and Acceptability of Welfare*

Item	WIN	Outer-city
(1) Below group mean for both orientations	33	41
(2) Above group mean for both orientations	19	13
Ratio of (1) to (2)	1.8	3.0
Number of respondents	163	175

The mean values indicate that the WIN fathers find quasi-illegal activities slightly more acceptable than do the outer-city fathers. Poor men who are in dire need of money and who live in areas where quasi-illegal activities flourish openly might be expected to react this way. What is surprising is that the poor men do not rate them even higher.

A substantial difference between poor and nonpoor fathers is observed in the correlations between life aspirations and work ethic on one hand and quasi-illegal activities on the other. Strong negative values appear for the WIN fathers, both white and black (see Table 5-5). There is a strong tendency for these fathers to see quasi-illegal activities as opposed both to "the good life" and to identification with work. The corresponding correlations for the outer-city fathers turn out to be near zero: the more affluent fathers see little relation between their acceptance of quasi-illegal activities and fulfillment of their life aspirations and work ethic. A likely interpretation of the findings is that quasi-illegal activities (at least in the form of the shoplifting or hustling listed in Orientation 4) are irrelevant to persons living in more middle-class settings; these are not realistic options to them. To poor persons living in poor neighborhoods, however, quasi-illegal activities present realistic options, and the choice of such activities bears directly on life goals and identification with work.

One similarity among the groups of fathers appears in the relation of acceptability of welfare to life aspirations and work ethic. No group seems to associate its own acceptance or rejection of welfare with its maintenance of life goals or self-identification with work, an interpretation based on the essentially zero correlations between Orientations 5 and 1 and 5 and 2 shown in Table 5-5.

The groups are also alike in their positive correlations between acceptability of welfare and lack of confidence. The fathers in each group who feel most insecure about their own abilities tend to find welfare most acceptable. Lack of confidence seems to incline male heads of household toward acceptance of welfare at all economic levels, although the tendency is stronger at the low level.

Orientations 6 and 7

The expressed tendencies of the men to work, even though they have what they consider sufficient money, and to get training to be able to earn more are much the same as those for the mothers and sons.

On Orientation 6, which measures the intention to work beyond the need for money, the mean values are similar among groups and relatively high, indicating that work holds an interest that goes beyond economic reward.

Whatever their race or welfare status, all the fathers show strong inclination to take training if they do not have enough money, as reflected in the high ratings they give to Orientation 7. The correlations between these intentions and the work ethic are substantial (see Table 5-5) for all except the outer-city black fathers, whose correlation is virtually zero. Perhaps they, like their wives and sons, are so concerned about being able to maintain their current status that they cannot conceive of training obtained while unable to support a family as self-developing.

Orientation 8

Ratings of the outer-city black fathers, like those of their wives and sons, show a distinct bias arising from the class status of the interviewers. The value of 2.72 reported for the 500 outer-city black fathers represents the averaging of the mean values of 2.17 given to lower-class interviewers and 3.26 given to middle-class interviewers. (The correlation between ratings and interviewers' class is 0.43.)

The interpretation applied to the wives and sons seems equally valid here: the fathers are very sensitive about their status and achievement. They are trying to impress middle-class interviewers with their success in the face of discrimination, while indicating to the lower-class interviewer that his lack of success results from inadequate effort rather than discrimination.

Summary and Conclusions

In certain ways this chapter merely reiterates the findings of the previous two chapters. Poor fathers, as well as poor mothers and poor sons, identify strongly with work, tend to reject quasi-illegal activities, and find welfare acceptable. A new finding is that both poor and nonpoor black fathers show great lack of confidence in their ability to succeed, whereas poor as well as more affluent white fathers are reasonably confident. Acceptability of welfare, on the other hand, follows economic rather than racial lines: poor whites and blacks have higher mean ratings on this orientation than do the more affluent blacks and whites.

The racial differences in the responses of the poor fathers must be taken as tentative because of the small number of cases. A further limitation is that the poor adult males in this study are all fathers who have decided to stay with their families. No responses are reported from men who have deserted their families or who maintain a way of life that never included supporting a family. One can only speculate, for example, about the work ethic of these men. Though it would be useful to have data on them, the lack of it is not crucial because of the data that have been obtained from poor youths on welfare, many of whom may become "street-corner" men who do not support their families. That these poor youths start with the same positive orientations as do more affluent youths indicates that a later loss of self-identification with work would be the result of environmental experiences, not of childhood rejection of the importance of work. This study illuminates the orientations of the potential "street-corner" men as well as of welfare fathers—knowledge of value in formulating public policy about the poor.

6

Work Orientations by Race and Status

MANY DIFFERENT FINDINGS about many groups have been reported in past chapters. This chapter seeks to relate the findings that reveal similarities and those that show differences in work orientations arising from race and socioeconomic status. It is not a summary of all previous findings, for it ignores the pattern of responses peculiar to certain groups to present broader trends.

The first step is to combine certain groups into larger units. Each unit is composed of both sexes, so that response differences between males and females are not reflected in the findings. To arrive at this, the responses from three groups not previously mentioned are included. The new groups are italicized in the following list.

Unit 1. 267 long-term black welfare mothers and 267 sons, and 122 short-term black welfare mothers and 122 sons.

Unit 2. 81 black WIN men, and 957 women.

Unit 3. 163 white WIN men, and 228 *women*.

Unit 4. 500 outer-city black mothers, 500 fathers, 250 sons, and 250 *daughters*.

Unit 5. 175 outer-city white mothers, 175 fathers, 100 sons, and 75 *daughters*.

The first unit is made up of the poorest black people—older mothers and their teen-age sons on welfare. Unit 2 is made of up mothers and fathers who are also on welfare, but who are younger than the adults in Unit 1 and who are participating in the Work Incentive Program (WIN). Unit 3 shifts to poor white people—white mothers and fathers in the WIN program; responses of the mothers appear here for the first time. Unit 4 consists of black outer-city intact families that have made it out of the ghetto. Responses of the daughters in these families appear here for the first time. Unit 5 contains the highest status persons in the study, white middle-class family members, with the responses of the daughters appearing for the first time.

Medians of mean values and correlation coefficients are reported for the units in Tables 6-1 and 6-2. These figures are derived from the responses of the subgroups in each unit. The median of the mean values given by welfare mothers and sons to the work ethic orientation, for example, is 3.32. (Appendix Tables c-6 and c-7 contain the mean values and correlations of each subgroup.) The medians for each unit on this orientation show that the poor and the nonpoor, blacks and whites, the young and the old, feel the same way about work. There appears to be no loss of identification with work for

TABLE 6-1. *Medians of the Mean Values Given Selected Work Orientations by Five Units of Respondents*

	Orientation					
Unit[a]	Life aspirations	Work ethic	Lack of confidence	Acceptability of quasi-illegal activities	Acceptability of welfare	Job discrimination
1. Black welfare mothers and sons	3.66	3.32	3.12	1.26	2.66	3.12
2. Black WIN trainees	3.68	3.42	2.76	1.25	2.36	2.88
3. White WIN trainees	3.66	3.36	2.54	1.24	2.18	2.50
4. Outer-city blacks	3.72	3.42	3.16	1.22	2.04	2.58
5. Outer-city whites	3.62	3.25	2.46	1.19	1.60	2.18

a. Breakdown of the units is given on p. 82.

either adult recipients of welfare or their children. If there is any trend in the data at all, it indicates a slightly less strong attachment to work on the part of the outer-city whites—specifically the sons and daughters (see Appendix Table c-6).

The median values for Orientation 1 indicate a common level of life aspirations among all units, and those for Orientation 4, a common rejection of quasi-illegal activities as a preferred source of income.[1] Not only do welfare recipients—black and white—identify with work, but their life aspirations are as high as those of employed persons and they wish to avoid legally marginal activities to the same extent.

Marked difference by race is seen for Orientation 8, which measures extent of belief in discrimination against blacks in the job market. Black welfare units give the highest median ratings, while the white outer-city unit gives the lowest. WIN whites fall in between these extremes, perhaps indicating a greater understanding than the more affluent whites of the difficulties faced by blacks in the work force. The black outer-city unit reveals only a slightly higher median

TABLE 6-2. *Medians of the Correlations between Selected Work Orientations and Characteristics for Five Units of Respondents*

	Orientation or characteristic		
Orientation and unit^a	Work ethic	Acceptability of welfare	Level of education
Lack of confidence			
1. Black welfare mothers and sons	0.29	0.26	−0.20
2. Black WIN trainees	0.24	0.32	−0.22
3. White WIN trainees	0.18	0.30	−0.24
4. Outer-city blacks	0.28	0.22	−0.18
5. Outer-city whites	0.15	0.10	−0.20
Acceptability of welfare			
1. Black welfare mothers and sons	...	...	−0.22
2. Black WIN trainees	...	...	−0.24
3. White WIN trainees	...	...	−0.18
4. Outer-city blacks	...	...	−0.18
5. Outer-city whites	...	...	−0.09

a. Breakdown of the units is given on p. 82.

rating than the white WIN unit, which is difficult to interpret because, as noted earlier, their ratings on Orientation 8 are greatly
influenced by interviewers' class status. It may be appropriate to say
that the black outer-city families have an ambiguous view of discrimination as it bears on work force advancement of blacks.

Racial differences are also shown in responses to Orientation 3,
which measures lack of confidence in one's ability to succeed. Regardless of status, whites show relatively high confidence in their
abilities (low ratings) while blacks show little confidence.

An adequate interpretation of racial difference in response requires
consideration of the set of correlation coefficients that measures the
relation between the work ethic and lack of confidence. Table 6-2
shows that the median correlation coefficients for the black units are
around 0.28; for the two white units, around 0.16. This survey of
the median correlations confirms the earlier findings: blacks with
the strongest work ethic tend to feel the least confident about their
own abilities. For whites, whether poor or affluent, there is much less
relation between the two orientations.

Two other differences follow lines of social-economic status rather
than of race. First, outer-city whites, with their superior social-
economic status, give the lowest ratings to acceptability of welfare.
The next lowest rating is given by outer-city blacks, whose status
is lower than that of outer-city whites but higher than that of welfare
groups. The other ratings, with the highest being given by the welfare mothers and sons, can be explained by economic status. The
second difference is found in the correlations in column 2 of Table
6-2, which indicate that only the high-status whites (unit 5) do not
associate strong feelings of insecurity with dependence on welfare.

Finally, in spite of the differences in ratings among units on acceptability of welfare and lack of confidence, the relation of these
ratings to level of education is the same. In the last column of Table
6-2, all units show negative correlations between education and these
two orientations. This indicates that among all persons, regardless
of race or status, one, or both, of the following is happening: (1) persons who are most confident and not dependent on welfare achieve

the highest levels of education; (2) a high level of education strengthens confidence and makes welfare less acceptable. The link between certain psychological orientations and educational level is common to all groups.

Interpretation of Results

Three possible interpretations of the data just presented are offered here. One emphasizes the caste, or racist, features of American society, another emphasizes the culture of poverty thesis, and the last emphasizes imperfect opportunity in the social system. The first explanation is that blacks' work orientations are different from those of whites as a result of pervasive segregation. Blacks, regardless of economic status, find themselves segregated within families, communities, schools, and jobs. Because life experiences occur within an all-black social system, the argument goes, orientations toward life in general and work in particular should be fundamentally different from those of white people.

One major flaw in the caste explanation is that feelings of insecurity are consistently high throughout the supposedly black caste system and low throughout the supposedly white one. If persons were competing within two separate systems, one would expect great lack of confidence among those of low status in each system. The uncertainty of the more affluent blacks suggests their concern about moving up to or staying within the middle class (as defined by the white majority), a concern that tends to militate against the caste explanation. A second flaw in this explanation is that if a true caste system existed one would expect some difference between blacks and whites in basic life orientations, including the nature and level of life aspirations and how strongly the work ethic is held. That these orientations are shared equally by blacks and whites throws doubt on the hypothesis.

What about the culture of poverty explanation? According to this view, all people who are poor share a common culture, which includes their basic orientations toward life. Responses from poor whites should therefore be similar to those of poor blacks. The data show, to be sure, certain similarities between these units, including self-identification with work, life aspirations, and the negative correlations of educational level with insecurity and welfare dependence. The difficulty is that these similarities are shared by the more affluent units as well. The poor do not exhibit a unique pattern of orientations. In addition, there are two marked differences between the poor black and poor white units. The latter exhibit much more confidence in their abilities and much less awareness of racial discrimination than the former. The explanation that different cultures account for the observed pattern of work orientations is not borne out by the findings of this study.

The third explanation, citing imperfect opportunity, overlaps the first, in that it recognizes the existence of certain castelike elements in American society, even though blacks and whites, poor and non-poor, share a common culture. These castelike elements restrict rather than completely block advancement. Being black in American society means not only being singled out and discriminated against in the job market (the high ratings of black respondents on the discrimination orientation bear witness to their recognition of this), but also having more difficulty obtaining adequate housing, education, health and other services than whites do. Hence, to be black is to have inferior opportunities, to have to function in situations that are less advantageous to advancement than those within which whites function. This is the chief reason that all blacks show a high level of insecurity. Even those who seem to be "making it" must continue to cope with adverse situational factors that do not affect white middle-class people to the same degree.

The success of some blacks, however, demonstrates that there is some opportunity for advancement. And achievement of a certain degree of affluence among blacks has a marked effect: they find welfare less acceptable than poor blacks, even less than poor whites. Responses vary along economic rather than racial lines.

A slightly different economic pattern is seen in the correlations relating lack of confidence to acceptability of welfare (see Table 6-2).

Those who are uncertain about their abilities, such as poor whites and blacks and outer-city blacks, tend to relate this insecurity to dependence on government support. This is a reasonable finding. Failure for those near the bottom of the economic ladder means a descent into (or continuation on) government-supported welfare. Failure for those at the higher level, such as the outer-city whites, is likely to mean not being promoted to a better position rather than failing so completely as to need welfare. The point is that the *magnitude* of the correlation between lack of confidence and acceptability of welfare follows economic rather than racial lines.

Neither the culture of poverty nor the caste explanation adequately accounts for the data summarized in this chapter. The preferred explanation, "imperfect opportunity," essentially says that the place of poor people and black people in our society is not fixed. While no strict caste system or major difference in culture separates the various segments of the population represented in this study, the data on orientations suggest that blacks face more difficulties in achieving upward mobility than whites do.

7

Work Orientations and
Work Activity

PREVIOUS CHAPTERS have interpreted the psychological and social meaning of work orientations held by various groups of the poor and nonpoor at a given point in time. This chapter takes up a more speculative issue: How are work orientations related to experiences in the work force? To answer this, the action model introduced in Chapter 1 is used.

According to the model, psychological orientations influence actions but are not the only determinants. Environmental conditions also affect action. And continuing encounters in the environment help shape not only people's orientations but also the kinds of subsequent situations they are likely to meet. Thus orientations are the product of past actions and at the same time guides for present action.

This study was designed to test certain features of the action model in the hope that, if the model proved valid, additional empirical data could be used to hypothesize a more detailed formulation of the relation between work orientations and work activity. This chapter therefore begins by testing the model and then hypothesizes its expansion based on additional data.

Testing the Model

Can at least one of the orientations measured in this study reasonably be said to directly influence the work activity of the poor? Does work experience—success or failure in work activity—in turn affect specific orientations? Making tests such as these necessitates examination of the correlations between work orientations and work activity. A prerequisite for such an examination is a specific definition and measure of work activity. This definition is based on the situation of trainees in the Work Incentive Program (WIN), for they are the one group in this study for which predictions can be made about work activity from earlier measures of work orientations.

Defining Work Activity

One obvious way of both defining and measuring the work activity of WIN trainees is to determine whether they are working at the time they leave, or are terminated from, the WIN program. It might be argued, however, that the mere fact of employment at one point in time is not convincing evidence of work activity. Poor persons often have patchy work histories, being employed for a few weeks and then unemployed for a time. Such transient members of the work force may have less positive work orientations than do more stable workers, and to give both types the same work activity rating might dilute any relation that could otherwise be found between work orientations and work activity. Some evidence of continuous effort in the work force should be included in the measure of work activity.

Fortunately, the WIN operation offers an automatic way of taking into account continuity of employment. A WIN trainee is terminated as "employed" only after he has been on the job for three to six months.[1] This length of time provides some assurance that the former trainee is not a transient participant in the work force. It might therefore seem reasonable to define and measure work activity by giving a score of 0 to the WIN trainee who has been terminated without a job, and a score of 1 to the trainee terminated with a job.

This simple dichotomized measure is adequate for a population, such as that of WIN trainees, of which a large number remain unemployed after termination from the program. Substantial proportions of both scores will appear in such a group. However, for a population in which virtually everyone is employed, such as the outer-city fathers, this measurement scheme is unsatisfactory, for almost all members will receive a score of 1. There would thus be no differentiation among individuals in the group and hence no possibility of distinguishing levels of work activity on the basis of scores on work orientations. While this study is primarily concerned with the work activity of poor people, a definition of work activity that is also applicable to the regularly employed is required if direct comparisons are to be made between the two groups of the effect of work orientations on activity.

If stability of employment should be taken into account in a measure of work activity, should length of employment itself be the general definition and measure? The difficulty with this approach is that, according to our action model, one could hardly expect to find a relation between orientations measured at one point in time and subsequent long-term activity that may itself influence work orientations. Length of employment should be a function of the experience of success or failure on a job, with this experience leading in time to more positive or more negative work orientations that in turn lead to continuation or termination of the job. Hence, an initial measure of work orientations should be predictive only of short-term work activity.

Arriving at a more general and useful concept of work activity requires some assumptions. The first is that, while "work activity" is partly staying on a job, it is also the amount of effort put into it. The second is that the money a person receives from a job is some indication of the amount of effort he is putting into it. Thus earnings become a measure of work activity. Applied to the WIN situation, these assumptions postulate that scores on at least one of the work orientations will be higher for trainees working at the time of termination and holding jobs that pay the highest wages, lower for those earning less (which might be the result of either a lower hourly wage or fewer hours worked a week), and lowest for those earning nothing.

The use of "dollars earned" as an index of work activity allows comparison between poor and affluent groups. It is as straightforward and valid to correlate the work-orientation scores of outer-city fathers with their earnings as it is to do so for WIN trainees. Another advantage of this measure is that it is readily interpretable in the feedback action model. High income can be viewed as being caused by positive work orientations and in turn encouraging them. In this study, therefore, job income will be used as an index of work activity. Income is graded on a ten-point scale in which 0 indicates no income and 9 indicates income of more than $300 a week.[2]

Establishing a measure of work activity makes it possible to examine correlations between that variable and work orientations, and to test the supposition that at least one orientation significantly, if not strongly, influences work activity. The most satisfactory group on which to test the model is the WIN mothers.

Orientations and Work Activity of WIN Women

Data on work orientations of the 1,439 WIN trainees were gathered initially during the spring of 1969. The time at which a trainee completed the work orientation questionnaire is denoted as T_1. During the spring of 1970 and again in the winter of 1971, the records of the same trainees were examined to determine whether they had been terminated from the program and, if so, their employment status and earnings. The time of termination of a trainee is denoted as T_2. Only about 60 percent (828) of the trainees had left WIN by the winter of 1971. After termination of trainees, attempts were made at four of the six study sites to reinterview them about their work orientations and views about the WIN experience. A total of 237 reinterviews (about 30 percent of those terminated) were completed by the spring of 1971. This second set of work orientations, obtained during reinterview, occur at time T_3. The task, then, is to analyze two sets of correlations: (1) between work orientations measured at time T_1 and work activity measured at time T_2; and (2) between activity at time T_2 and orientations at time T_3.

Only the black WIN women constituted a large enough group to make the complete analysis significant. By winter of 1971, 551 black women of the original group had been terminated from WIN. At time of termination, 214 of them had been employed for about six months, and 337 had been terminated without employment.[3] Of these 551 women, 188 were reinterviewed. At time of reinterview, 11 who had been employed at termination were no longer working, while 16 who had been unemployed at termination were working. The orientations of these 27 women at reinterview were influenced by both work and nonwork experiences, making ambiguous any interpretation of the influence of success or failure in the work world on orientations. These reinterviews were therefore dropped from the analysis, leaving 161 reinterviews of women who were either working or not working at both times: termination from WIN (T_2) and reinterview (T_3).

According to data presented in Table 7-1, the work activity of all 551 terminated WIN women is most heavily influenced by two characteristics with which they enter the program—their finding welfare acceptable and their educational level. The -0.20 and 0.18 correlations between work activity and these two factors, respectively, are the largest for any of the initially measured work orientations and personal characteristics. It should be noted, however, that these correlations, while significant statistically, are not very large; the multiple correlation between these variables taken together and work activity is 0.25. Correlations of the magnitude of 0.20 suggest that being in the WIN program does not completely counteract the negative influence on work activity of initially strong dependence on welfare and low levels of education.

The strength of these relationships probably would be greater if certain conditions were not attenuating the results. Trainees in the WIN program are not a random sample of all welfare recipients, but a special group of recipients who have been judged "appropriate" for

TABLE 7-1. *Correlations between Work Activity at Time* T_2 *and Orientations and Personal Characteristics of Black WIN Terminated Women at Time of Entry into the Program* (T_1) *and Reinterviewed Women at* T_1 *and* T_3[a]

Orientation or characteristic	Time T_1 All terminated women	Time T_1 Reinterviewed women	Time T_3 Reinterviewed women
1. Life aspirations	0.10	0.10	...[b]
2. Work ethic	0.03	0.05	−0.08
3. Lack of confidence	−0.06	−0.05	−0.16
4. Acceptability of quasi-illegal activities	−0.06	0.03	...[b]
5. Acceptability of welfare	−0.20[c]	−0.21[c]	−0.39[c]
6. Work beyond need for money	−0.05	−0.01	−0.11
7. Train to improve earning ability if poor	0.09	0.08	0.15
8. Job discrimination	0.01	0.09	−0.06
Age	0.08	0.08	...
Educational level	0.18[c]	0.32[c]	...
Number of children	0.04	0.03	...
Years on welfare	−0.10	−0.01	...
Number of women	551	161	161

a. T_1 is the time at which work orientations initially were measured; T_2 the time at which work activity (dollars earned) was measured for terminated women; T_3 the time at which work orientations were remeasured for the portion of the terminated women who were reinterviewed.

b. Not measured.

c. Significantly different from zero beyond the 0.01 level of probability.

referral, and this may be lowering the observed relationships. Recipients with the lowest education and the greatest dependence on welfare may be precisely those who are not referred to WIN. Correlations computed for a group that is considered more work-ready than welfare recipients in general are likely to be lower than those that would have been obtained from a group not specially chosen. This kind of reasoning also would explain the essentially zero correlation between the number of children WIN mothers have and their work activity. Only welfare recipients who had adequate day care for their children were thought "appropriate" for entry into WIN, a selectivity that probably lowers the correlation between work activity and number of children.

Another reason for the relatively weak relationship between welfare dependence and work activity may be in events between T_1, when orientations were measured, and T_2, when work activity was measured (almost two years in some cases). The training effort in WIN itself, or other experiences during the period between the two measurements, may have blunted the relationship. If so, and if one applies the feedback model, a much stronger correlation between work activity at T_2 and the welfare dependence measure at T_3 would be expected. That is, a stable history of working (or not working) during a period of six months to a year should have a major effect on the acceptability of welfare orientation. Table 7-1 shows this correlation for the 161 reinterviewed WIN women to be a substantial -0.39. (This correlation might result in part from the influence of welfare dependence at T_1 on this variable at T_3. When the effect of welfare dependence at T_1 is controlled, however, the correlation between work activity and welfare dependence at T_3 is still a significant -0.33.)

From the correlations observed in Table 7-1, it is reasonable to infer a substantial interaction between welfare dependence measures and work activity. But is it equally reasonable to state that welfare dependence at T_1 influences work activity, and that work activity influences welfare dependence at T_3? The premise adopted here is that explicit statements about influence are inferences from theoretical and empirical evidence rather than undisputed "facts." The significant correlations between variables, while one of the necessary conditions to support an inference of influence, are not in themselves sufficient to do so.

Another issue is the time at which the variables exert their influence. Can the influencing variable be said to operate before the variable supposedly influenced? In the case of the WIN women there is no ambiguity. Welfare dependence measured at T_1 was clearly in operation before work activity at WIN termination, and the subsequent degree of welfare dependence, at T_3, clearly existed after termination from WIN. Still another issue is, Are the variables under consideration perhaps not directly related at all, but instead influenced in the same direction by a third variable? There is no foolproof way of ruling out this possibility of error in attributing influence. One can only attempt to include in the correlational analysis all the relevant variables. On the basis of current data this source of error does not seem to be present. (One might, for example, consider educational level as a third variable. The correlations, however, between welfare dependence and work activity at time T_1 or T_3 are still significant when educational level is controlled: -0.17 and -0.36, respectively.) The last point is that no other data or theory refutes the possibility of the influence sequence proposed. These arguments make it eminently reasonable to infer that welfare dependence at least partially influences work activity, and that subsequent work experience partially influences welfare dependence. Hence the basic process of the feedback action model is substantiated.

The significant correlation between level of education and work activity can be interpreted, by using the same arguments, as a causal relationship. That is, the level of education achieved before entrance into WIN directly influences trainees' subsequent work activity. This finding is consistent with our model, exemplifying the situation mentioned in Chapter 1 whereby actions of an earlier time, such as graduating from high school, create a favorable situation for occupational advancement at a later time. A diagram of the influence on work activity of educational level, a social achievement variable, and acceptability of welfare, a psychological variable, is shown in Figure 7-1.

An important question is whether there is mutual influence between the sociological and the psychological variables, and Table 7-2 shows that there is, in fact, a correlation of -0.17. (This is not shown in Figure 7-1, because there is no way of determining the direction of the influence arrow between the two variables.) The WIN mothers had completed their formal education long before their welfare dependence was measured, making indeterminate any causal relationship. A large number of one group of respondents, the Baltimore welfare sons, were still in school. Analysis of their ratings on acceptability of welfare by grade level raises the possibility that strong

FIGURE 7-1. *Sequence of Influence Linking Acceptability of Welfare and Level of Education to Work Activity, Terminated and Reinterviewed Black WIN Women*

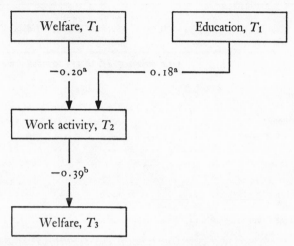

a. Correlations based on responses from all 551 terminated women.
b. Correlation based on responses from the 161 terminated women who were reinterviewed.

feelings of dependence encourage early school dropout.[4] But without more data, this possibility must be treated cautiously.

Expanding the Model

Only one orientation has been found to have a direct influence on work activity. Does this mean that other orientations are psychologically unrelated to it? Not if they are linked to work activity through the acceptability of welfare orientation. The first step in expanding the model, therefore, is to consider correlations between scores on the welfare orientation and on other orientations measured at the same time. According to Table 7-2, lack of confidence is the most strongly associated with acceptability of welfare at both times T_1 and T_3. Since nothing suggests that a third variable causes the correlations, nor do other data or theories argue against an influence linkage, such a linkage seems reasonable. By the same logic the work

TABLE 7-2. *Selected Correlations and Intercorrelations among Work Orientations, Education, and Work Activity, Terminated and Reinterviewed Black WIN Women*

Orientation or characteristic	Life aspirations	Work ethic	Lack of confidence	Acceptability of welfare	Education	Work activity at T2
	Orientations at T1, *all 551 terminated women*					
Correlations						
Life aspirations	...	0.21[a]	0.02	−0.06	−0.01	0.10
Work ethic	...	...	0.19[a]	0.01	−0.07	0.03
Lack of confidence	...	...	...	0.31[a]	−0.11[a]	−0.06
Acceptability of welfare	...	...	...	...	−0.17[a]	−0.20[a]
Education	...	...	...	...	...	0.18[a]
Partial correlations						
Acceptability of welfare, controlled for education	...	...	...	...	...	−0.17[a]
Education, controlled for acceptability of welfare	...	...	...	...	...	0.15[a]
	Orientations at T3, *161 reinterviewed women*					
Correlations						
Work ethic	...	...	0.31[a]	−0.04	−0.12	−0.08
Lack of confidence	...	...	...	0.34[a]	−0.28[a]	−0.16
Acceptability of welfare	...	...	...	...	−0.17	−0.39[a]
Partial correlations						
Acceptability of welfare at T3, controlled for acceptability of welfare at T1	...	...	...	...	...	−0.33[a]
Acceptability of welfare at T3, controlled for education	...	...	...	...	...	−0.36[a]
	Orientations at T1 *correlated with Orientations at* T3, *161 reinterviewed women*[b]					
Correlations						
Work ethic	...	0.18[a]	0.05	−0.02	...	...
Lack of confidence	...	0.06	0.36[a]	0.17	...	...
Acceptability of welfare	...	0.03	0.17	0.43[a]	...	...
Partial correlation						
Lack of confidence, controlled for acceptability of welfare	...	...	...	0.05	...	...

a. Significantly different from zero beyond the 0.01 level of probability.

b. For purposes of this section of the table, the stubs concern orientations at T1, the column headings orientations at T3.

ethic may be plausibly regarded as linked to lack of confidence and life aspirations as linked to the work ethic.

A major difficulty arises, however, in attempting to fix the direction of influence among orientations. All orientations were measured together, whether at T_1 or T_3, and there is no way of establishing their temporal priority. The data do not explicitly indicate whether at T_1 acceptability of welfare, for example, is influenced by or influencing the other orientations (that is, in a diagram, arrows from the other orientations might point either toward or away from acceptability of welfare). This uncertainty calls for an assumption: when work activity is initiated, when welfare recipients attempt to train for and enter the work force, influence on the extent of this activity originates in life aspirations and moves through work ethic to lack of confidence to welfare dependence. The effect of the success or failure of the work effort, on the other hand, flows back along these linkages from welfare dependence to life aspirations. A further attempt to enter the work world would again be influenced by the psychological sequence beginning with life aspirations and flowing through acceptability of welfare. The hypothesized feedback model of how orientations influence work activity is shown in Figure 7-2.

While the directions of the influence arrows in portions of the diagram cannot be definitively established, it is possible to show that the sequence in Figure 7-2 is consistent with Blalock's approach to determining causal sequences.[5] The rationale of the approach is that if variable A influences B, which in turn influences C, then all the influence of A on C is absorbed by B and the partial correlation between A and C with B's effect controlled is zero. That is, correlations between adjacent variables should be high but correlations between variables separated by one or more variables should be zero when the effects of the intervening variables are controlled.

A correlation of 0.17 is shown, for example, in Table 7-2 between lack of confidence measured at time T_1 and acceptability of welfare measured at time T_3 for the 161 reinterviewed trainees. This correlation should disappear when the effect of T_1 on T_3 is taken into account. And indeed, the partial correlation between lack of confidence

FIGURE 7-2. *Sequence of Influence Linking Work Orientations and Work Activity, Terminated and Reinterviewed Black WIN Women*[a]

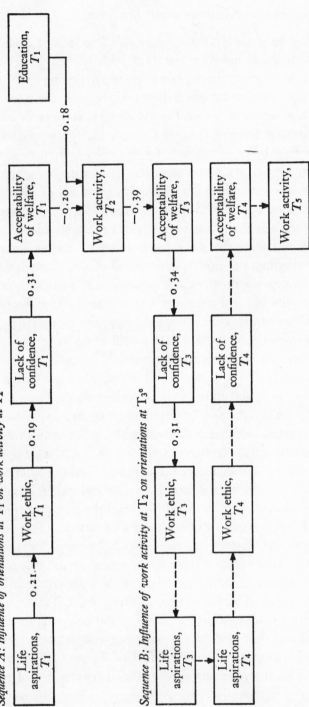

Sequence A: Influence of orientations at T_1 on work activity at T_2[b]

Sequence B: Influence of work activity at T_2 on orientations at T_3[c]

a. All measured orientations are not included in this diagram. Those for which the information provided was not sufficient to justify further complexity in the diagram have been omitted.

b. Correlations based on responses of all 551 terminated women at T_1.

c. Correlations based on responses of 161 reinterviewed women at T_3.

at T_1 and acceptability of welfare at T_3 with the effect of the welfare orientation at T_1 controlled is virtually zero. This kind of argument by no means decisively establishes the validity of the overall sequence seen in Figure 7-2. Further research is needed to test it.

The sequence suggests that poor women's high life aspirations and strong work ethic actually contribute to their lack of confidence in their own abilities, and this in turn makes them accept welfare more readily and "give up" on work effort. This theory contrasts sharply with the simplistic view that expressed goals and overt actions are directly connected. The simplistic view, which probably is held by many middle-class persons, is that if a poor person expresses a strong work ethic he will be working regularly. It does not take account of the complex interaction among orientations and how they are influenced by environmental experiences. According to our model and data, work ethic is unrelated to work activity. It is a strong disposition to accept welfare that influences work activity. And this disposition in turn is the result not of low aspirations or low work ethic, but rather of a series of failures to obtain a decent job.

The Impact of Success and Failure

The correlational analysis in Table 7-2 and the influence sequence immediately surrounding work activity in Figure 7-2 suggest that the outcome of the WIN program for trainees—success or failure in obtaining a job—affects certain of their orientations toward work. To assess the specific nature of this effect, Table 7-3 gives the mean values for orientations at times T_1 and T_3, and the differences between them, for the reinterviewed women who were either employed or unemployed after their termination from WIN.

The first set of data indicate that the 92 trainees who failed to obtain jobs after termination from WIN not unreasonably felt greater dependence on welfare and even less confidence in themselves than they did at the start of their training. (The rating on the acceptability of welfare rose 0.24 point and that on insecurity rose 0.16 point.[6]) Adherence to the work ethic, perception of job discrimination, and intentions to work beyond the need for money were essentially un-

TABLE 7-3. *Mean Values on Orientations at Entrance to and Termination from WIN, Reinterviewed Women*[a]

Orientation	Unemployed from termination to reinterview			Employed from termination to reinterview		
	T₁	T₃	T₃ minus T₁	T₁	T₃	T₃ minus T₁
Work ethic	3.46	3.42	−0.04	3.48	3.37	−0.11
Lack of confidence	2.75	2.91	0.16	2.74	2.73	−0.01
Acceptability of welfare	2.39	2.63	0.24	2.08	2.05	−0.03
Work beyond need for money	2.87	2.96	0.09	2.84	2.86	0.02
Train to improve earning ability	3.72	3.57	−0.14	3.79	3.80	−0.01
Job discrimination	2.91	2.86	−0.05	3.08	2.75	−0.33
Number of women	...	92	...	...	69	...

a. Entrance to WIN is denoted as T_1; time of reinterview as T_3.

changed; this development is consistent with the view that orientations of this kind, far removed from work activity in the influence pattern depicted in Figure 7-2, are not much affected by it.

While employed terminees might well be expected to express less dependency and more self-confidence, the successful work experience has not led to changes in these orientations, according to the data. This essential stability, however, is a marked contrast to the increased dependency and lack of confidence of those who remained without jobs.

A time factor may be at work here. When women who have participated hopefully in a training program fail to obtain employment, they have an immediate experience of failure in the work world and so immediately become more dependent on welfare. On the other hand, even with a job, women who have been on welfare may feel uncertain about their tenure or about the adequacy of their salary to improve their standard of living. Thus their orientations show no positive change in the short run, although it would be hypothesized that such changes would occur with time as the women remained on the job and received regular raises.

A change is observed in one of the orientations that one would expect, on the basis of the model, to be unrelated to work activity.

Employed terminees decrease their rating on the job discrimination scale by −0.33. It is understandable that blacks who obtain jobs give less credence to the belief that blacks cannot get jobs because of discrimination. This change in belief apparently has little effect on the work activity–orientation sequence proposed here. But experience gained through work may have important psychological effects that are not related to the extent of work activity as such. Alleviation of the feeling of being discriminated against may help people relate more effectively to others in various aspects of life, and this is important, aside from its effect on work activity.

An assumption that underlies this discussion of the reinterview data should be stated explicitly: the major difference among WIN terminees is their employment status. Without control groups and a broader research effort, this assumption cannot be verified. It is possible that another variable is responsible for the differences in ratings. Higher welfare dependence and insecurity on the part of unemployed terminees may be a function of their having to return to welfare (95 percent of the unemployed terminees were back on welfare; 5 percent were supported by their husbands). Perhaps women who fail in the work force would not feel more dependent on welfare if the alternative source of income were support from a husband or some welfare system more benign than the one that currently exists.

This study does not permit separation of the effect of work force failure from that of returning to complete dependence on a welfare system that probably violates the self-respect of its clients. The data do make clear, nevertheless, that termination from WIN without a job aggravates the welfare dependence of women and tends to discourage their work force participation. The WIN program may thus be counterproductive by making a substantial proportion of its trainees less employable than when they entered the program.[7]

Orientations and Work Activity of Black Welfare Mothers and Sons

To further support the influence sequence in Figure 7-2 and to ascertain that it is not merely the result of chance fluctuations in correlation coefficients, responses of another welfare group of fam-

ilies headed by women—the long- and short-term welfare mothers—
were analyzed. (The two groups were combined to increase the number of respondents and hence the stability of the correlations among
variables.) At the time data were collected in Baltimore, mothers
receiving Aid to Families with Dependent Children (AFDC) were
not encouraged to work because any earnings were deducted from
their welfare payment. Nevertheless, about 18 percent of the 389
mothers were employed.

Data on income and on orientations were gathered at the same
time. It is hard to say, therefore, whether the orientations influence
work activity, as measured by dollars earned, or vice versa. Our
model, in any case, shows a continuing feedback effect, which makes
it less important to specify the direction of the influence arrows than
to examine the structure of the sequence itself, to determine which
orientations affect work activity. To facilitate comparison with the
sequence for WIN women, the influence arrows are pointed in the
same direction. Figure 7-3 shows the sequence for Baltimore welfare
mothers, and Table 7-4 the correlations between orientations, work
activity, and education. Both are based on the premise used for the
WIN women—that strongly correlated variables should be adjacent
to each other, while unrelated variables are farther away.

The sequence for the Baltimore welfare mothers is essentially the
same as that for WIN women. Acceptability of welfare and educational level are the major predictors of dollars earned. The multiple
correlation between work activity, as measured by job earnings, and
the two significant predictors is 0.31. That a similar work orientation
sequence is shown by two different groups of female heads of household adds to the credibility of the sequence, although it does not
prove its validity.

In the earlier discussion of how the work orientations of welfare
mothers affected those of their sons, substantial correlations were
shown between the ratings of mothers and of sons on several orientations, including the work ethic, lack of confidence, and acceptability
of welfare. Does this influence encourage or discourage the sons from
obtaining employment?

Of a total of 389 long- and short-term welfare sons in this study,

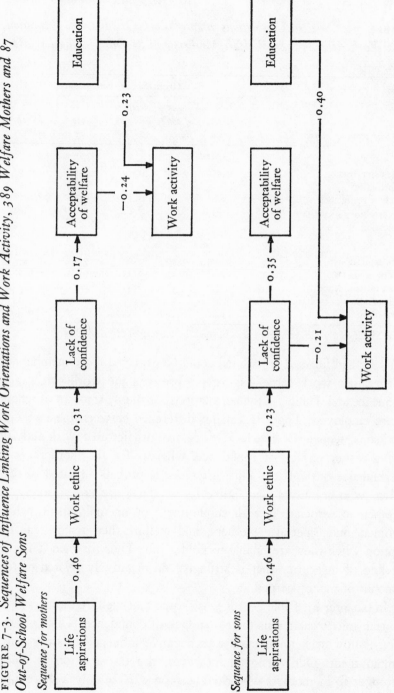

FIGURE 7-3. Sequences of Influence Linking Work Orientations and Work Activity, 389 Welfare Mothers and 87 Out-of-School Welfare Sons

Sequence for mothers

Life aspirations — 0.46 — Work ethic — 0.31 — Lack of confidence — 0.17 — Acceptability of welfare — 0.23 — Work activity
Education
—0.24 — Work activity

Sequence for sons

Life aspirations — 0.46 — Work ethic — 0.23 — Lack of confidence — 0.35 — Acceptability of welfare
Education — 0.40
—0.21 — Work activity

TABLE 7-4. *Selected Correlations among Work Orientations, Education, and Work Activity, 389 Welfare Mothers and 87 Out-of-School Welfare Sons*

	Orientation or characteristic				
Orientation or characteristic	Work ethic	Lack of confidence	Acceptability of welfare	Education	Work activity
Mothers					
Life aspirations	0.46ᵃ	0.15ᵃ	0.09	−0.02	0.01
Work ethic	...	0.31ᵃ	0.08	−0.04	0.07
Lack of confidence	...	...	0.17ᵃ	−0.19ᵃ	−0.08
Acceptability of welfare	...	...	...	−0.18ᵃ	−0.24ᵃ
Education	...	...	...	...	0.23ᵃ
Sons					
Life aspirations	0.46ᵃ	0.26ᵃ	0.08	−0.12	−0.14
Work ethic	...	0.23	0.15	−0.04	−0.04
Lack of confidence	...	...	0.35ᵃ	−0.21	−0.21
Acceptability of welfare	...	...	...	−0.17	−0.13
Education	...	...	...	...	0.40ᵃ

a. Significantly different from zero beyond the 0.01 level of probability.

only 87 had finished school and could be expected to be members of the regular work force. Figure 7-3 presents the work orientation sequence and Table 7-4 the correlations for the 87 sons, 46 of whom were employed. There is a major difference between the mothers' and sons' sequences. The largest negative predictor of work activity for the sons is lack of confidence, whereas for the mothers, it is dependence on welfare. This difference is probably related to sex. Men, who are usually ineligible for welfare, are not as likely as women to associate it with employment or unemployment, while women, and especially mothers, find welfare their major realistic option when they are unable to hold a job. Thus for men it is the feeling of insecurity that is strongly and negatively related to the amount of money earned.

In Chapter 4 (Table 4-6) it was shown that welfare mothers tend to transmit to their sons their own lack of confidence. This orientation is now seen to function as a negative influence on their sons' employment. Oddly enough, however, the transmission is much stronger from mothers who have been on welfare only a short time (one year) than from long-term welfare mothers, suggesting that it is not extensive welfare experience as such that causes this transmission. Probably the insecure socioeconomic conditions in which the poor find themselves are the deciding factor. And these conditions exist not only for those on welfare, but also for mothers who have been struggling to keep off it and for some outer-city black households. The high level of insecurity transmitted to the outer-city black sons may draw some of them out of the work force, leading eventually to downward mobility from the quasi-middle-class status of their parents.

The transmission of positive feelings about acceptability of welfare from both short- and long-term welfare mothers does not directly affect the sons' work activity, but the evidence mentioned in note 4 to this chapter about in-school welfare sons does suggest that high ratings on welfare dependence may lead to early school termination. That welfare mothers also transmit a strong work ethic to their sons does not offset the disadvantages of the lack of confidence and welfare dependence they transmit. Indeed, a strong work ethic tends to increase insecurity.

The mother-to-son transmission of work orientations appears to foster low work performance by the sons. Presumably, the mothers' influence occurs early in life. Perhaps the sons have both strong work ethic *and* insecurity before their school or work experience. In other words, lack of confidence, rather than being influenced by the work ethic, may develop right along with it. On the other hand, the maternal influence may be reinforced by the children's experiences in the ghetto, and the link between work ethic and lack of confidence may be strengthened by school and work experience.

James Coleman, as part of a national study of educational opportunity, asked students a few questions that are similar to those used in this study to measure lack of confidence. Coleman found not only that black students' ratings increased between the sixth and ninth grades, but also that high feelings of insecurity about their ability to succeed had a negative correlation with verbal achievement on standardized tests.[8] According to the Coleman data, the farther black students go in school, the farther they fall behind whites in verbal achievement.[9] Such lesser achievement among blacks at the same grade level as whites may itself increase lack of confidence.

High feelings of insecurity on the part of black school-age children may be a result of what some claim is their lack of inherent intellectual ability. This study provides no data on intellectual ability as such, nor is there any solid scientific evidence of innate intellectual differences between whites and blacks.[10] It seems unreasonable to attribute the 18 percent school dropout rate for the 389 welfare sons in this study, as against 3 percent for the 100 outer-city sons, to inherent ability differences, when situational factors in ghetto life are known to militate against continuance in school. There is, moreover, strong evidence of the major structural imperfections in the educational system that frustrate the potential achievement of the poor. Data from other studies show how the operation of schools penalizes the lower-class students.[11]

All this should not obscure this study's finding that poor mothers transmit their own lack of confidence and acceptability of welfare orientations, creating further obstacles to their sons' academic and work achievement.

Orientations and Work Activity of Black and White Outer-City Fathers

To further test the credibility of the influence sequence, sequences exhibited by other heads of household—the black and white outer-city fathers—were drawn. The work orientation sequences for both are presented in Figure 7-4 and the correlations in Table 7-5.[12]

The striking feature of the sequence for black outer-city fathers is its essential similarity to that of the out-of-school welfare sons. Significant predictors of work activity are educational level and lack of confidence. The multiple correlation coefficient is 0.33. Fathers with the least confidence are earning the least money. Acceptability of welfare again bears no direct relation to work activity, supporting the earlier interpretation that men are less likely than women to connect the two.

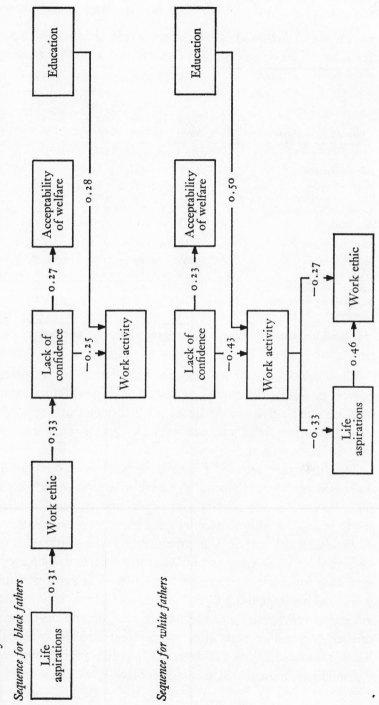

FIGURE 7-4. *Sequences of Influence Linking Work Orientations and Work Activity, 462 Black and 170 White Outer-City Fathers*

Sequence for black fathers

Sequence for white fathers

TABLE 7-5. *Selected Correlations among Work Orientations, Education, and Work Activity, 462 Black and 170 White Outer-City Fathers*

	Orientation or characteristic				
Orientation or characteristic	Work ethic	Lack of con- fidence	Accepta- bility of welfare	Educa- tion	Work activity
Black fathers					
Life aspirations	0.31[a]	0.09	0.00	−0.03	0.02
Work ethic	...	0.33[a]	0.03	−0.22[a]	−0.06
Lack of confidence	...	...	0.27[a]	−0.37[a]	−0.25[a]
Acceptability of welfare	...	...	...	−0.17[a]	−0.13[a]
Education	...	...	...	...	0.28[a]
White fathers					
Life aspirations	0.46[a]	0.24[a]	−0.04	−0.19[a]	−0.33[a]
Work ethic	...	0.16	−0.08	−0.14	−0.27[a]
Lack of confidence	...	...	0.23[a]	−0.26[a]	−0.43[a]
Acceptability of welfare	...	...	...	−0.08	−0.10
Education	...	...	...	...	0.50[a]

a. Significantly different from zero beyond the 0.01 level of probability.

The work orientation sequence for white fathers shows differences as well as similarities to that of the black fathers. Educational level and insecurity again are the major predictors of work activity. The strong influence of educational level on income sends the multiple correlation up to 0.59.

The differences are two. First, strong work ethic does not lead to decreased confidence. Second, there are substantial negative correlations between work activity and life aspirations and activity and work ethic (the influence arrows for these two orientations point away from work activity), meaning that as white fathers earn more money, their work ethic and life aspirations decline. Increased affluence may influence white fathers to lower their identification with work and their goals in life. Without data from other groups of affluent white fathers and further research on the development of orientations, this interpretation must be treated as highly speculative. There is also a difference of degree. While educational level and lack of confidence influence the earnings of black as well as white fathers, education is of much greater help to whites, who translate educational attainment into income much more readily than blacks. This finding is consistent with national census data.[13]

Summary and Conclusions

Two empirical findings in this chapter are of special importance. First, the more acceptable welfare is to black mothers when they enter the WIN program, the lower their work activity after termination from the program. Second, the WIN mothers who terminate the program without a job find welfare more acceptable than they did when they entered the program. These and related findings support our feedback action model by showing that at least one work orientation directly influences work activity, and the outcome of this activity—failure in the work world—has a feedback effect on that orientation. (Success in the work world does not have a short-run effect but should have one in the long run.)

In a more speculative part of the chapter, the action model is expanded and possible influence linkages between the other orientations and acceptability of welfare are presented. The expanded model suggests that poor women's lack of confidence makes welfare more acceptable, and that confidence, in turn, is diminished by a strong work ethic and high life aspirations. That is, attempting to maintain middle-class standards decreases poor women's confidence in themselves.

The low work activity of welfare women is a result not of their rejecting the significance of work, but of their continually experiencing failure in the work world and thus finding welfare an acceptable alternative.

Examination of correlations between work activity and work orientations for men show that the lack of confidence orientation, rather than acceptability of welfare, is most strongly related to work activity, probably because welfare is not a possible source of income for most men, while the feeling of insecurity is directly relatable to lesser work force activity.

8

Do the Poor
Want to Work?

To be effective, welfare and manpower policies for the poor must be based on knowledge of how poor people view life and work. Evidence from this study unambiguously supports the following conclusion: poor people—males and females, blacks and whites, youths and adults—identify their self-esteem with work as strongly as do the nonpoor. They express as much willingness to take job training if unable to earn a living and to work even if they were to have an adequate income. They have, moreover, as high life aspirations as do the nonpoor and want the same things, among them a good education and a nice place to live. This study reveals no differences between poor and nonpoor when it comes to life goals and wanting to work.

This conclusion may seem somewhat paradoxical. If poor persons, especially welfare recipients, really regard work as important for their self-esteem, why are they not working and moving out of poverty? Why are welfare rolls increasing rather than decreasing?

The paradox would be easily explained if one could show that the poor covered in this study were merely giving responses they thought middle-class persons wished to hear, but the data as adjusted for respondent bias give little evidence of gross distortion. Instead, the implicit behavioral theory on which the paradox is based must be considered. It assumes a direct connection between the goal of self-respect through work and actual work activity. Such a theory may fail to explain events because it is too simple—goals and actions are not necessarily linked directly. Actions tend to be guided most strongly by orientations that emphasize beliefs and intentions.

Thus, for black women on welfare the orientation that is directly linked to work activity combines belief and intention elements and measures acceptability of welfare. Women who find welfare most acceptable tend to show the lowest work activity. By itself, this finding might suggest that poor women prefer welfare to work. The data also indicate, however, that ratings on this orientation are sensitive to encounters in the work world. Women in the Work Incentive Program (WIN) who were terminated from it without jobs—who experienced another failure in the work world—showed a marked increase in the acceptance of welfare score over their score when they entered WIN, demonstrating that the concrete experience of failure directly and negatively influenced this work orientation. The picture that emerges is one of black welfare women who want to work but who, because of continuing failure in the work world, tend to become more accepting of welfare and less inclined to try again. Given this insight, what should policy be on requiring welfare mothers to work?

Work Requirements for Welfare Mothers

Common arguments for proposing a work requirement are that work is psychologically valuable for welfare mothers and provides a model for their children. The data indicate that even long-term welfare mothers and their teen-age sons, though the sons have spent virtually their entire lives on welfare, continue to have a strong work ethic and do not need to be taught the importance of work. To encourage welfare mothers to enter the work force, it is necessary to present them with a chance to experience success in jobs that will support them. But realistically, what are the chances of training large numbers of welfare mothers so they can support their families above the poverty level?

The background characteristics of the average welfare mother—
only ten years of education, three children, no husband, and various
chronic illnesses[1]—do not encourage the hope that many of them can
achieve economic independence. Despite this, considerable government effort has gone into the attempt to train welfare recipients for
jobs. About 1.6 million welfare cases eligible for the WIN program
had been reviewed by local departments of welfare across the nation
between August 1968 and April 1970. These included fathers and
out-of-school teen-agers receiving Aid to Families with Dependent
Children (AFDC), but the great majority were mothers (95 percent
of all adult AFDC recipients). Only about 10 percent of the 1.6 million eligibles were considered suitable for enrollment in WIN.[2] Of
all those who had been terminated from WIN by April 1, 1970, only
about 20 percent had jobs. Hence, the WIN program was successful
in getting jobs for only about 2 percent (10 percent times 20 percent)
of the total eligible welfare population; this during a period when
welfare rolls for the whole country were rising by about 40 percent.
The median wage for the employed WIN women was around $2 an
hour, hardly sufficient to support a family of four adequately.[3]

While various excuses can be made for the WIN program, its performance has been sufficiently poor to demonstrate the improbability
of training and placing in the regular job market any substantial number of the more than 2.7 million mothers currently receiving welfare.
(The overall job placement record for WIN as of February 1971 was
still only 20 percent.[4]) A work requirement for welfare mothers
could mean pushing more of them through the WIN program even
though 80 percent would not obtain jobs in the open market or it
could mean forcing them to fill the lowest-paid jobs in our society,
those paying far below the minimum wage.[5] Neither of these solu-
tions is desirable. Just as failure in the WIN program increases
mothers' acceptability of welfare, working in jobs that do not pay
them enough to support their families is likely to reinforce just those
psychological orientations that characterize the poor and discourage
them from further work activity.

It is in this context that the latest federal efforts to provide public service employment for welfare recipients should be judged.[6] If these jobs provide dignity, training, and sufficient income, they can be of help to the poor. If the jobs are ill-paid and regarded by employers and employees as "make-work," they may prove even more discouraging to the poor than no jobs at all. Welfare recipients who want training and jobs should not be denied the opportunity, but the training and support should be of the quality that makes occupational success a reasonable probability.

The consequences of failure in the work world should be considered not only from the point of view of the mothers, but from that of their children as well. The data suggest that poor black mothers have a substantial influence on the work orientations of their sons, including those measuring acceptability of welfare and lack of confidence, and that the sons' adherence to these two orientations may lead to both early school dropout and low work activity. Hence, stringent work requirements for welfare mothers, which are likely to lead to additional experiences of failure, can psychologically damage not only the mothers but also their children.

Mothers who are unable to support themselves and their families can be supported at a decent level by public funds without fear of damage to their work ethic or that of their sons. If the support is given, as Gilbert Steiner has suggested, "in a framework of honorable dependency,"[7] it will carry with it no social stigma, and the recipient mothers and children may be less likely to suffer from the feeling of inadequacy that inhibits subsequent work activity. But welfare payments, honorable or otherwise, are unlikely to be large enough to enable families to move up to middle-class circumstances—they serve only as a holding measure. The opportunity to move up would be enhanced if there were two breadwinners in the family rather than one, so an intact family has a potential economic advantage.

Moving Up

A striking feature of the outer-city black families in this study, who have made it out of the ghetto, is that their economic viability often depends on the joint income of husband and wife. The husbands, with only a tenth grade education on the average, are working at jobs that are not much different from those of men in the WIN program or men still in the ghetto. The outer-city blacks, however, despite having the high level of insecurity common to poor blacks, have stayed on their jobs. And most important, they have stayed married to women who on the average have an eleventh grade education and bring in almost 30 percent of the family income. The implication for policy here is that efforts to eliminate poverty should include incentives for a husband and wife to stay together as a family unit.

Job training for the poor might be thought of in family terms. Special benefits could be given to a husband and wife who participated in programs to gain new skills that would qualify them for jobs providing substantial joint income. At the same time, special efforts could be made to help the children of these adults succeed academically. Day care with a strong educational component for preschool children might serve the dual purpose of freeing a mother to work if she wished and providing special benefits to the child. In view of the negative results of past governmental efforts to aid the poor, such as WIN, however, one cannot help questioning whether such programs would really help.

A more equitable distribution of the tax burden would probably have greater economic effect than governmental "training" programs. If the poor were to pay a much lower proportion of their income in taxes than do the affluent,[8] they would have more money to pay for training or day care themselves. Additional subsidies could be paid directly to heads of families who worked full time yet did not earn enough to move out of poverty.

Income is not the only issue involved in a family's moving out of poverty. There is a psychological component as well, to judge from the responses of the outer-city black family members. Both the outer-city parents and their children show lack of confidence and extreme consciousness of their marginal social status. The psychological stress of moving from lower to middle class may be great, and not every poor person may want or be able to accommodate to it. The situation may be especially difficult for the father who has less education than his wife and knows that he, unlike his white counterpart, can by himself barely support his family in middle-class status. This man is known to have a great lack of confidence in his abilities, and those with high scores on the lack of confidence orientation earn the least income. Why these outer-city black men remain with their families and work hard to support them, while others with similar educational background do not, is a question of fundamental significance to which insufficient research has been directed.

In any case, attempts to help people overcome poverty and achieve social mobility should recognize the interplay between psychological and economic factors. An increase in family income of a few hundred dollars a year may in theory be enough to raise a family above some economically defined "poverty line." But such an amount is unlikely to generate a burst of confidence that would enable them to transform the ghetto into a better place to live or leave it for a better neighborhood. While a substantial rise in income might encourage some families to decide to move to a middle-class neighborhood, such a decision would not be a purely economic one: it would also be based on perceptions of ability to succeed. This study has clearly pointed to the tendency of poor blacks to be very uncertain about their ability. The limitation of using economic measurements alone is that they may show many rising above poverty because of government transfer payments, when socially and psychologically the urban ghettos remain unchanged.

The foregoing is not a criticism either of economic analysis or of proposals for guaranteeing income to the poor, but should provide a basis for moving beyond the often-expressed concern that transfer payments to the poor may take away their incentive to work.[9] Excessive concern that a relatively low level of guaranteed income—around the poverty level—would cause people to drop out of the work force reflects a misunderstanding of the life and work orientations of the poor. They are no more likely to settle for this meager income and cease working than are middle-class people. Preliminary results from a work incentive experiment with low-income (intact) families, conducted by the University of Wisconsin, support this view.[10]

The plight of the poor cannot be blamed on their having deviant goals or a deviant psychology. The ways in which the poor do differ from the affluent can reasonably be attributed to their different experiences of success and failure in the world. There is ample evidence to suggest that children who are born poor face discriminatory barriers to advancement in the educational and occupational worlds,[11] which thrust them into failure much more consistently than their middle-class counterparts.

Appropriate policies would enable more poor people to experience success. While success cannot be guaranteed, the probability of its attainment for larger numbers of the poor might be increased in two ways. The first is to lessen the risk of failure by removing discriminatory barriers so that, for example, more poor people become eligible for better jobs; the second, to reduce the cost of failure, when it does occur, by providing a guaranteed income at least a small margin above the poverty level. Poor families should be given enough economic security and low-risk opportunity to rise in status, according to their desire and ability, without being overwhelmed by failure induced by inequities in the social system.

Appendix A

The Questionnaires

Home Interview Version of the Work Orientation
Questionnaire as Administered to Long- and
Short-Term Welfare Mothers and Sons and
Outer-City Families, Baltimore, Maryland

Interview Number _____

I

Everybody has some idea about the best kind of life and the worst kind of life for himself. I have some statements about things that might happen in life. I also have a sheet to give you [HAND RESPONDENT WHITE PAGE] which has a picture of a ladder on it. The top of the ladder says *Best way of life* and the bottom says *Worst way of life*. The steps of the ladder are numbered from 1 to 4. I will read a statement and you are to choose the numbered step that says how much the activity described is part of the best or worst life *as you see it*. "4" means that the activity perfectly fits the best way of life for you and "1" means that it perfectly fits the worst way of life. You can choose any number on the ladder for each statement I read.*

Rating

1. The first activity is "Having fun—having a good time."
Where would you put this on the steps—what number would
you choose?...................................... _____

* For a picture of the ladders used, see the self-administering version of the questionnaire.

   2. Getting respect from your friends...................... ————
   3. Staying out of trouble with the law.................... ————
   4. Living in a place where you *don't* get along with your neigh-
      bors... ————
   5. *Not* having enough money to buy the things you want..... ————
   6. Having a regular job............................... ————
   7. Helping other people............................... ————
   8. Being in poor health............................... ————
   9. Having difficulties with your family................... ————
  10. Being honest...................................... ————
  11. Having a job that is well-paid........................ ————
 12a. [MALES ONLY] *Not* able to support a wife and family...... ————
 12b. [FEMALES ONLY] Having a husband who does not support you
      and your family.................................. ————
  13. Having a job that you do *not* like.................... ————
  14. Getting along with your neighbors..................... ————
  15. *Not* caring about other people...................... ————
  16. Having a job that pays very little..................... ————
  17. Owning an expensive car............................ ————
  18. Being famous...................................... ————
  19. Having good health................................. ————
  20. Having very little education......................... ————
  21. Having plenty of money to get what you want........... ————
  22. Having a job that you like........................... ————
  23. *Not* helping to make this a better world.............. ————
  24. Your friends do *not* respect you..................... ————
  25. Getting along well with your family................... ————
  26. Having important goals in life....................... ————
  27. Being poor.. ————
 28a. [MALES ONLY] Supporting a wife and family............. ————
 28b. [FEMALES ONLY] Having a husband who supports you and
      your family...................................... ————
  29. Working only some of the time....................... ————
  30. Being dishonest.................................... ————
  31. Having a nice place to live and plenty of food........... ————
  32. Having very little fun in life......................... ————
  33. Being in trouble with the law........................ ————
  34. Making this a better world to live in.................. ————
  35. Having a good education............................ ————
  36. Having *no* important goals in life.................... ————
  37. Cannot afford an expensive car....................... ————

38. *Not* being famous..................................... _____

38a. What else would be part of the best life for you? _____

_____

38b. What else would be part of the worst life for you? _____

_____

39. We have talked about the things that make up the best and worst life. Think now of your own life *at the present time.* Where would you place it on this same ladder—which numbered step indicates where you *now* stand in life?......... _____

39a. [IF RATINGS 1 THRU 3] Why didn't you place your present life higher on the steps?
[IF RATING 4, GO TO QUESTION 39b]

_____

_____

39b. [IF RATINGS 2 THRU 4] Why didn't you place your present life lower on the steps?
[IF RATING 1, GO TO QUESTION 39c]

_____

_____

39c. What do you need to do in order to move up the steps?

_____

_____

39d. What kinds of things are you now doing that you think will help you move up?

_____

_____

[TAKE BACK LADDER ON WHITE PAGE]

II

I now have some questions about ways of getting enough to live on that would be the best or worst *for you.* I also have another picture of a ladder. [HAND RESPONDENT YELLOW PAGE] This time the top says *Best way of getting enough to live on* and the bottom says *Worst way of getting enough to live on.* I will mention an activity and you are to choose the step that says how much that activity is the best or worst way *for you* to get enough to live on. You can choose any number on the ladder for each statement I read.

Rating

40. Borrowing money from your friends. _____
41. Having the government find you a good job. . . . . _____
42. Having a job such as washing dishes. . . . . _____
43. Having a job where you learn some special skills. . . . . _____
44. Gambling. . . . . _____
45. Being on welfare. . . . . _____
46. Having a job that doesn't pay much but you are sure of keeping the job. . . . . _____
47. Having a job where you need a lot of education. . . . . _____
48. Having a job that pays a lot of money but there is a lot of hard physical work. . . . . _____
49. Having a job with clean working conditions. . . . . _____
50. Having a job that your friends respect. . . . . _____
51. Running numbers. . . . . _____
52. Having a job where you could become famous. . . . . _____
53. Having a job where you earn a lot of money but the work is very dirty. . . . . _____
54. Peddling stolen goods. . . . . _____
55. Having the government send you enough money every week. _____
56. Owning a small business. . . . . _____
57. Having a job that pays a lot of money but you will be fired if you don't work hard. . . . . _____
58. Having the government give you a decent place to live and enough food and clothing. . . . . _____
59a. [MALES ONLY] Having a wife who brings in money. . . . . _____
59b. [FEMALES ONLY] Having a husband who brings in money. . . _____
60. Having a job with dirty working conditions. . . . . _____
61. Having a job where you are let go when business is slow. . _____
62. Being a successful shoplifter. . . . . _____
63. Having a job where you direct a lot of other people. . . . . . . _____
63a. What other activities would be the *best* way for you to get enough to live on? _____
63b. What other activities would be the *worst* way for you to get enough to live on? _____

[TAKE BACK LADDER ON YELLOW PAGE]

III

I now have a few questions about what a person might do if certain things happen. I also have another picture of a ladder. [HAND RESPONDENT PINK PAGE] The top says *Certainly would do that* and the bottom says *Never would do that*. For each question I read, please tell me which step on the ladder says how much you might do what is mentioned. You can choose any number on the ladder for each question I read.

Rating

64. Suppose you inherited enough money so that you and your family could live comfortably without your ever working, would you go ahead and work anyway?.................. _____
65. How do you think your best friend would answer that question—what step would (he/she) choose?............... _____
66. Suppose the government sent you as much money every week as you could get by working at a regular job. And suppose you could keep the government money even if you continued in that job. Would you go ahead and work anyway?.. _____
67. How do you think your best friend would answer that question—what step would (he/she) choose?............... _____

IV

Suppose that you could *not* earn enough money by working to support yourself or your family; using the ladder, tell me how much you might do each of the following things:

Rating

68. Go on welfare?....................................... _____
69. Get more education, if you were paid enough while learning? _____
70. Leave your family?.................................... _____
71. Enter a job-training program, if you were paid enough while in training?.. _____
72. Make money at hustling or gambling?.................. _____

V

If your best friend could not earn enough money to support himself or his family, how much do you think (he/she) might do the following things:

Rating

73. Go on welfare?....................................... _____
74. Get more education, if paid enough while learning?....... _____

75. Leave (his/her) family?............................. ——
76. Enter a job-training program, if paid enough while in training? ——
77. Make money at hustling or gambling?.................. ——

[SECTION VI TO BE ASKED ONLY OF ADULT WOMEN;
FOR OTHER RESPONDENTS GO TO SECTION VII]

VI

If you were on welfare, how much might you do each of the following things:

Rating

78. Go to work if there was a good place to leave your children
while you were away?.............................. ——
79. Go to work if you could keep everything you made up to
$150 per month without losing welfare payments?........ ——
80. Go into a job-training program if your welfare allowance
remained unchanged?.............................. ——
81. Go to work if the job was close to home?.............. ——
82. Go to work if such jobs as house-cleaning or waiting on tables
at a restaurant became available?...................... ——

VII

83. How much money do you feel you need a week in order to
live comfortably?................................——

[TAKE BACK LADDER ON PINK PAGE]

VIII

I have some statements which say certain things about work. I also have another picture of a ladder which now says *Agree* at the top and *Disagree* at the bottom. [HAND RESPONDENT BLUE PAGE] I will read each statement and you tell me which numbered step on the ladder says how much you agree or disagree with the statement. You may choose any number on the ladder for each statement I read.

Rating

84. To me, a very important part of work is the opportunity to
make friends...................................... ——
85. Getting recognition for my own work is important to me.. ——
86. Work should be the most important part of a person's life. ——
87. Success in an occupation is mainly a matter of knowing the
right people...................................... ——

88. It is better to be poor than to make a living by breaking the law... _____
89. Most people like to work.............................. _____
90. I would like my family to be able to have most of the things my friends and neighbors have........................ _____
91. I like to work...................................... _____
92. Racial discrimination is a major reason why Negroes don't get good jobs.. _____
93. Work is a way of being of service to God.............. _____
94. I like to direct the work of others.................... _____
95. A man really can't think well of himself unless he has a job.. _____
96. The main satisfaction a person can get out of work is helping other people.. _____
97. To me, it's important to have the kind of work that gives me a chance to develop my own special abilities............. _____
98. A person should constantly try to succeed at work even if it interferes with other things in life..................... _____
99. Success in an occupation is mainly a matter of luck....... _____
100. Sometimes it may be right for a person to lose friends in order to get ahead in work............................... _____
101. If I don't have a regular job, I don't feel right........... _____
102. A Negro with a good education has much *less* chance of getting a good job than a white person with the same education _____
103. Work is most satisfying when there are hard problems to solve... _____
104. It is highly desirable for a teen-age girl to learn some skills so that she can get a good job later on.................... _____
105. Work is a good builder of character.................... _____
106. Even if you dislike your work you should do your best.... _____
107. To me, gaining the increased respect of family and friends is one of the important rewards of getting ahead in an occupation.. _____
108. To me, it's important in an occupation to have a chance to get to the top.. _____
109. It is more desirable for a mother with small children to stay at home than to go out to work...................... _____
110. In order to get ahead in a job you need to have some lucky breaks... _____
111. Most jobs in private business are routine and dull........ _____
112. Most women who draw welfare prefer to work.......... _____
113. Success in an occupation is mainly a matter of hard work.. _____

114. It is more important for a job to have the respect of family and friends than to provide a lot of money............... ———

115. Hard work makes you a better person.................. ———

116. It's important for me to have a job where there is a lot of responsibility... ———

117. In general, I don't like to work...................... ———

118. Drawing welfare for a long period of time makes a person feel worthless....................................... ———

119. I like the kind of work you can forget about after the work day is over.. ———

120. Work should *not* be a very important part of a person's life.. ———

121. To me, it's important in an occupation that a person be able to see the results of his own work.................... ———

122. Success in an occupation is mainly a matter of how much you know.. ———

123. To me, almost the only thing that matters about a job is the chance to do work that is worthwhile to society......... ———

124. Work should *not* interfere with a person's family life...... ———

125. To be really successful in life, you have to care about making money... ———

126. In order to be successful in a job, people have to like you... ———

127. I feel good when I have a job........................ ———

128. It is more important to get along with your friends and family than to work hard at a job........................... ———

129. To me, work is nothing more than a way of making a living. ———

130. It is important for me to have a job that makes my community a better place to live in............................. ———

131. Work is *not* generally satisfying to me.................. ———

132. The most important part of work is earning good money.. ———

133. A person has to like his work in order to do a good job... ———

134. Work helps you forget about your personal problems..... ———

135. It's important to do a better job than the next person...... ———

136. It's *not* very important to have a job where you can learn new skills... ———

137. You should help other people on a job so that they will help you... ———

138. Without a job you are nobody....................... ———

139. Success in an occupation is mainly a matter of how much effort you put into it............................... ———

[TAKE BACK LADDER ON BLUE PAGE]

IX

There are just a few more questions I want to ask you.

140. How old are you to your nearest birthday?............ _____
141. Are you now married?........................ No–1　Yes–2
142. What was the last grade in school that you completed?..._____
143. Are you now attending school?................. No–1　Yes–2
    [IF YES, ASK QUESTION 143a; IF NO, GO TO QUESTION 144]
143a. What is the name of the school? _____
144. Are you now attending a job-training program?..... No–1　Yes–2
    [IF YES, ASK QUESTION 144a; IF NO, GO TO QUESTION 146]
144a. What kind of training are you getting? _____

_____

145. How long (how many weeks) have you been in the pro-
    gram?.. _____
146. Have you attended any trade school or job-training
    program in the past?........................ No–1　Yes–2
    [IF YES, ASK QUESTION 146a; IF NO, GO TO QUESTION 147c]
146a. What was the name of the last program? _____

_____

146b. When did you start—what month and year?........... _____
147. How long (how many weeks) were you in the program?._____
147a. What kind of training did you get? _____

_____

147b. Why did you leave? _____

_____

147c. What ways do you now get enough to live on? _____

_____

[IF A JOB IS MENTIONED, GO TO QUESTION 149;
IF NO JOB IS MENTIONED, ASK QUESTION 148]
148. Are you *now* holding a job?.................... No–1　Yes–2
    [IF YES, ASK QUESTION 149; IF NO, GO TO QUESTION 155]
149. About how many hours do you work a week?......... _____
150. How long have you had this job?................... _____
151. About how much do you earn a week?............. _____

151a. What do you do in this job? _____

_____

152. Do you hold another job besides the one just mentioned?...................................... No–1   Yes–2
[IF YES, ASK QUESTION 152a; IF NO, GO TO QUESTION 155]
152a. When did you start this other job—what month and year?. _____
153. About how many hours do you work a week?......... _____
154. About how much do you earn a week?.............. _____
154a. What do you do on this job? _____

_____

155. Have you had a job previously?.................. No–1   Yes–2
[IF YES, ASK QUESTION 155a;
IF NO, THANK RESPONDENT AND TERMINATE]
155a. When did you start that job—what month and year?..... _____
156. About how many hours did you work a week?......... _____
157. How long did you have that job?.................... _____
158. About how much did you earn a week?.............. _____
158a. What did you do on that job? _____

_____

158b. Why did you leave? _____

_____

159. Have you had a job before that one?............ No–1   Yes–2
[IF YES, ASK QUESTION 159a;
IF NO, THANK RESPONDENT AND TERMINATE]
159a. When did you start that job?........................ _____
160. About how many hours did you work a week?......... _____
161. How long did you have that job?.................... _____
162. About how much did you earn a week?.............. _____
162a. What did you do on that job? _____

_____

162b. Why did you leave? _____

_____

163.* How long have you lived at this address? _____

* Asked of outer-city respondents only.

164.* Where did you live before moving to this address? _____

_____

Not in Baltimore–0   Downtown–1   Other inner city–2
Middle ring–3   Outer ring–4

165.* How long did you live there? _____

166.* How many children are now living in your household? _____

[THANK RESPONDENT AND TERMINATE]

_____ _____ _____ _____ _____
Start   Finish   Date   Person Interviewed   Interviewer's Name

Self-Administering Version of the Work Orientation Questionnaire as Completed by WIN Trainees

An Opinion Survey

INTRODUCTION. *The following questions are being asked of WIN trainees in programs around the country. The purpose is to see how trainees look at life. This is* not *a test. There are no right or wrong answers. We only want your opinions about certain things that might happen in life. You should find these questions interesting. Please answer them as frankly and honestly as possible.*

Part I

Listed below are some statements which talk about things that might happen in life. At the right is a picture of a ladder which says *BEST way of life* at the top and *WORST way of life* at the bottom. The steps in between are numbered from "1" to "4." You are to consider which numbered step indicates how much you see each statement as part of the best or worst way of life. "4" means that you think the statement describes the very best way of life and "1" means that you think it describes the very worst way of life. Insert in the space provided after each statement the number you choose. You can choose any number on the ladder for each statement.

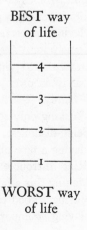

BEST way
of life

—4—

—3—

—2—

—1—

WORST way
of life

* Asked of outer-city respondents only.

Rating

Getting respect from your friends............................. _____

Staying out of trouble with the law.......................... _____

Living in a place where you *don't* get along with your neighbors.. _____

Not having enough money to buy the things you want.......... _____

Having a regular job... _____

Helping other people... _____

Being in poor health... _____

Having difficulties with your family......................... _____

Being honest... _____

Having a job that is well-paid............................... _____

[MALES ONLY] *Not* able to support a wife and family............ _____

[FEMALES ONLY] Having a husband who does not support you and
      your family.. _____

Having a job that you do *not* like........................... _____

Getting along with your neighbors............................ _____

Not caring about other people............................... _____

Having a job that pays very little........................... _____

Owning an expensive car...................................... _____

Being famous... _____

Having good health... _____

Having very little education................................. _____

Having plenty of money to get what you want.................. _____

Having a job that you like................................... _____

Not helping to make this a better world..................... _____

Your friends do *not* respect you............................. _____

Getting along well with your family.......................... _____

Having important goals in life............................... _____

Being poor... _____

[MALES ONLY] Supporting a wife and family.................... _____

[FEMALES ONLY] Having a husband who supports you and your
      family .... _____

Working only some of the time................................ _____

Being dishonest.. _____

Having a nice place to live and plenty of food............... _____

Being in trouble with the law................................ _____

Making this a better world to live in........................ _____

Having a good education...................................... _____

Having *no* important goals in life........................... _____

Part II

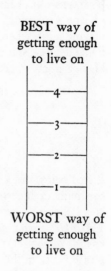

BEST way of
getting enough
to live on

Listed below are some statements which mention ways of getting enough to live on. At the right is another picture of a ladder. This time the top says *BEST way of getting enough to live on* and the bottom says *WORST way of getting enough to live on*. Again, the steps in between are numbered from "1" to "4." For each statement, please write the number you choose.

WORST way of
getting enough
to live on

Rating

Borrowing money from your friends.......................... _____

Having the government find you a good job.................. _____

Having a job such as washing dishes....................... _____

Gambling.. _____

Being on welfare... _____

Having a job that doesn't pay much but you are sure of keeping the job.. _____

Having a job that pays a lot of money but there is a lot of hard physical work. .... _____

Having a job with clean working conditions.................. _____

Having a job that your friends respect...................... _____

Running numbers... _____

Having a job where you could become famous................ _____

Having a job where you earn a lot of money but the work is very dirty.. _____

Peddling stolen goods..................................... _____

Having the government send you enough money every week..... _____

Having a job that pays a lot of money but you will be fired if you don't work hard.. _____

Having the government give you a decent place to live and enough food and clothing.. _____

[MALES ONLY] Having a wife who brings in money............. _____

[FEMALES ONLY] Having a husband who brings in money........ _____
Having a job with dirty working conditions.................. _____
Having a job where you are let go when business is slow....... _____
Being a successful shoplifter............................... _____
Having a job where you direct a lot of other people........... _____

Part III

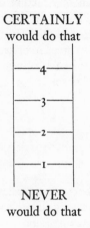

CERTAINLY
would do that

—4—

—3—

—2—

—1—

NEVER
would do that

Listed below are a few questions about what a person might do if certain things happened. At the right is another picture of a ladder which says *CERTAINLY would do that* at the top and *NEVER would do that* at the bottom. For each question, please write in the number you choose.

Rating

Suppose you inherited enough money so that you and your family
   could live comfortably without your ever working, would you go
   ahead and work anyway?............................... _____
How do you think your best friend would answer that question—
   what number would (he/she) choose?..................... _____
Suppose the government sent you as much money every week as
   you could get by working at a regular job. And suppose you
   could keep the government money even if you continued in that
   job. Would you go ahead and work anyway?................ _____
How do you think your best friend would answer that question—
   what number would (he/she) choose?..................... _____
Suppose that you could *not* earn enough money by working to support yourself or your family; using the ladder, tell me how much you might do
   each of the following things:
Go on welfare?... _____
Get more education, if you were paid enough while learning? .... _____
Leave your family?..................................... _____

Enter a job-training program, if you were paid enough while in
    training?... _____
Make money at hustling or gambling?........................ _____
If your best friend could not earn enough money to support himself or his
    family, how much do you think (he/she) might do the following things:
Go on welfare?... _____
Get more education, if paid enough while learning?............ _____
Leave (his/her) family?.................................... _____
Enter a job-training program, if paid enough while in training? ... _____
Make money at hustling or gambling?........................ _____

Part IV

AGREE

Listed below are some statements which say certain
things about work. At the right is another picture of
a ladder which says *AGREE* at the top and *DISA-
GREE* at the bottom. Again, the steps in between
are numbered from "1" to "4." For each statement,
please write in the number you choose.

—4—

—3—

—2—

—1—

DISAGREE

Rating

To me, a very important part of work is the opportunity to make
    friends... _____
Getting recognition for my own work is important to me....... _____
Work should be the most important part of a person's life....... _____
Success in an occupation is mainly a matter of knowing the right
    people.. _____
It is better to be poor than to make a living by breaking the law.. _____
Most people like to work.................................. _____
I like to work... _____
Racial discrimination is a major reason why Negroes don't get good
    jobs.. _____
I like to direct the work of others.......................... _____
A man really can't think well of himself unless he has a job..... _____
The main satisfaction a person can get out of work is helping other
    people.. _____

To me, it's important to have the kind of work that gives me a chance to develop my own special abilities................... _____

A person should constantly try to succeed at work even if it interferes with other things in life............................. _____

Success in an occupation is mainly a matter of luck............ _____

If I don't have a regular job, I don't feel right................. _____

A Negro with a good education has much *less* chance of getting a good job than a white person with the same education........ _____

It is highly desirable for a teen-age girl to learn some skills so that she can get a good job later on............................ _____

Work is a good builder of character......................... _____

Even if you dislike your work you should do your best......... _____

To me, gaining the increased respect of family and friends is one of the important rewards of getting ahead in an occupation....... _____

To me, it's important in an occupation to have a chance to get to the top... _____

It is more desirable for a mother with small children to stay at home than to go out to work................................. _____

In order to get ahead in a job you need to have some lucky breaks.. _____

Most women who draw welfare prefer to work............... _____

Success in an occupation is mainly a matter of hard work....... _____

It is more important for a job to have the respect of family and friends than to provide a lot of money..................... _____

Hard work makes you a better person....................... _____

It's important for me to have a job where there is a lot of responsibility... _____

Drawing welfare for a long period of time makes a person feel worthless... _____

I like the kind of work you can forget about after the work day is over... _____

To me, it's important in an occupation that a person be able to see the results of his own work............................. _____

Success in an occupation is mainly a matter of how much you know. _____

To me, almost the only thing that matters about a job is the chance to do work that is worthwhile to society.................... _____

To be really successful in life, you have to care about making money.. _____

In order to be successful in a job, people have to like you....... _____

I feel good when I have a job.............................. _____

To me, work is nothing more than a way of making a living..... _____

It is important for me to have a job that makes my community a better place to live in. . . . . _____

The most important part of work is earning good money. . . . . _____

A person has to like his work in order to do a good job. . . . . _____

You should help other people on a job so that they will help you. _____

Without a job you are nobody. . . . . _____

Success in an occupation is mainly a matter of how much effort you put into it. . . . . _____

Appendix B

Methodology of the Study

A PILOT STUDY of the work orientations of the poor was undertaken before the larger study reported in this volume because it was not clear from previous research whether significant, reliable, and unbiased data could be obtained on this topic. The pilot effort began in September 1967 with a series of tape-recorded discussions about work with four groups of five trainees each in one of the work-training programs in the District of Columbia.[1] Each of five sessions lasted about two hours. Open-ended questions about attributes of the best and worst ways of life and best and worst ways of getting an income were answered by the participants. Structured questions, rated on an agree–disagree ladder, were also answered.[2] Responses to both kinds of questions were discussed by the participants. The project director often had to do little but ask the questions as group members talked and argued about the meaning and significance of the items and the responses of others in the group.

Comments of these poor young men and women (in their late teens and early twenties) indicated that many of the structured and open-ended questions were tapping significant goals and beliefs about work and were well understood. From this experience an interview schedule was constructed which contained structured rating items and open-ended questions about life

1. For a report on the pilot study, see Leonard Goodwin, "Orientation of the Unemployed and Underemployed Poor Toward Work and Income Maintenance: A Feasibility Study" (Brookings Institution, April 1968; processed).

2. A number of the structured questions were taken from an earlier Brookings study of the occupational goals of regularly employed people. See Franklin P. Kilpatrick, Milton C. Cummings, Jr., and M. Kent Jennings, *The Image of the Federal Service* (Brookings Institution, 1964), pp. 275–76.

goals and occupational goals, beliefs about ways of achieving occupational success as well as the best and worst ways of getting enough to live on, and intentions about working if one had enough money.

Personal interviews were completed in late 1967 and early 1968 with almost 200 persons: poor teen-agers in New Haven; welfare mothers and their teen-age sons in Baltimore; poor teen-agers in Hickory Hill (not its real name), a small community adjacent to the District of Columbia; and a small group of middle-class teen-agers in a suburb of the District of Columbia. Responses to the open-ended questions were content-analyzed. Ratings on the structured items were factor-analyzed to see if certain sets of items clustered together to form psychologically significant scales. Several scales did appear in the analysis, indicating that the items were being answered in a consistent manner.

The forty-three poor male teen-age respondents from Hickory Hill were of special interest. Before the pilot study, an in-depth participation-observation study of all male teen-agers in Hickory Hill had been carried out by Derek Roemer.[3] He was able, on the basis of his research, to identify fifteen youths who belonged to the most delinquent peer groups in the community, and who were habitually involved in illegal activities and in trouble with the police. Twenty-eight other teen-agers were known to be oriented toward middle-class standards of life. The delinquent youths were expected to be much less work oriented than this group. All forty-three were interviewed by a teen-ager indigenous to the community who had been trained in interviewing during Roemer's study. The delinquent youths did indeed show less commitment to employed work and more interest in illegal activities than middle-class-oriented teen-agers.[4] These findings encouraged the belief that the items themselves were significant and the responses relatively unbiased.

Responses from thirty-six mothers who had been on the Baltimore welfare rolls at an earlier time were also examined. The finding that they were much more concerned about the money work provides than were women in the regular work force seemed to indicate realistic, unbiased responses, inasmuch as they had very low incomes. Most of the mothers who were still receiving welfare, as determined from the Department of Welfare records, admitted it when asked about their present source of income. These mothers and their teen-age sons responded to a structured item that indicated discrimination as a reason why blacks could not get good jobs. Even to white inter-

3. "Adolescent Peer Group Formation in Two Negro Neighborhoods" (Ph.D. dissertation, Harvard University, 1968).

4. Leonard Goodwin, "Work Orientations of the Underemployed Poor: Report on a Pilot Study," *Journal of Human Resources*, Vol. 4 (Fall 1969), pp. 508–19.

viewers, black respondents gave much higher ratings to this item than white respondents. These bits of evidence, along with others mentioned in the pilot study report, indicated that respondents were answering in an unbiased fashion and giving their actual views.

Another facet of the pilot study entailed asking about one-third of the respondents to explain the ratings they gave to the structured items. Their remarks were taken down verbatim by the interviewers, and helped identify the items that were well understood or misunderstood by both poor and non-poor persons. The participants in the pilot study clearly seemed to take the term "work" to mean employed activity and not other forms of making money, such as running numbers.

Overall results from the pilot study indicated the feasibility of developing a set of questions about work that would be understood by poor and nonpoor persons, that had adequate reliability, and that could be answered without marked bias. These findings set the stage for the effort reported in the main text.

Construction of the Work Orientation Scales

Following the analysis of pilot study results, two methodological steps were taken. First, the open-ended questions about work were turned into structured rating items. For example, the response "good health" was frequently given to the open-ended question about the attributes of the best life. "Good health" thereupon became one of the items to be rated on a four-step ladder ranging from "Best way of life" down to "Worst way of life."

Second, an explicit attempt was made to classify items according to psychological content. The basic distinctions were made analytically. It was assumed that people's goals in life and work—the state of affairs they wish to attain—could be examined separately from their beliefs about how to achieve those goals, so the items measuring life and occupational goals were distinguished from items measuring beliefs about ways of achieving them. All rating items created from open-ended questions about best and worst way of life were regarded as goal items, but all rating items constructed from open-ended questions about best and worst ways of getting enough to live on were classified as belief items because they discuss ways of reaching occupational or monetary success.

Two additional analytic separations of items were made. Items that explicitly posed action choices, or intentions, in a given context were regarded as having a psychologically different dimension than goals or beliefs. Finally, items asking about liking or disliking work were seen as a fourth dimension, which was not necessarily related to the others. Ten new items were created to measure affective reaction, or attitude, toward work. Further discussion of the rationale of these psychological elements appears in Chapter 1 and note 27 to that chapter.

When the research effort reported in the main text began in the fall of 1969, there were 140 rating items to measure the several psychological elements—attitude, goals, beliefs, intentions. After 120 long-term welfare mothers and their sons had been interviewed in Baltimore, an analysis was made of the new data. As a first step in constructing reliable measures of the psychological elements, a factor analysis was carried out on each set of items measuring a particular element.

Thus separate analysis of all the goal items revealed that positive life goals formed one scale and the occupational goal of self-development through work another. Both scales in turn were separate from that indicating money as an occupational goal. Analysis of the belief items yielded separate scales measuring acceptability of quasi-illegal activities on one hand and acceptability of welfare on the other. Intention items split into three scales, as discussed in the main text. The attitude items were analyzed separately, and only some of the ten items formed a unidimensional scale.

A few additions and deletions of items were made on the basis of this new preliminary analysis. (The home interview questionnaire in Appendix A was derived at this point and used in all ensuing home interviews.) As additional groups, including the outer-city groups, were interviewed, additional analyses were made to establish that the items were clustering in approximately the same way as they had for the welfare group.

After about 2,000 poor and nonpoor women and 1,400 poor and nonpoor men and youths had completed the work orientation questionnaire, a factor analysis for each group was carried out. In them all the 102 items that had been found to be consistent measures of the psychological elements were pooled. These last two factor analyses, as well as the earlier ones, were conceived solely as preliminary steps for appropriately clustering items. No assumptions were made about the ultimate reality of the factors themselves. During the last two analyses the aim was to allow all the items measuring the various elements to cluster together to obtain measures of work orientations.[5] The BMD University of California factor analysis program, which includes a principal components solution and orthogonal Varimax rotations, was used. The communality estimates included in the diagonal of the correlation matrix were the squared multiple correlation coefficients. The num-

5. The items constituting each element continued to cluster together in these two factor analyses of all items.

ber of factors rotated consisted of the number of eigen values having the value of 1 or more. (Inasmuch as only 80 variables could be included in this factor analysis program, three factor analyses were actually run for the male and three for the female groups. The items were overlapped to provide an opportunity for the items constituting each psychological element to appear with the items of the other elements.)

The steps for selecting the final set of 65 items used in this study for measuring work orientations were as follows.

1. All items that loaded about 0.30 or more on one of the rotated factors and did not have higher loadings on another factor were regarded as candidates for measuring a given orientation.

2. The intercorrelations among all the candidate items for a given orientation were examined. Items with relatively low intercorrelations which would not increase the reliability of the scale were dropped. Items also were dropped when they showed substantial correlations with items belonging to other scales.

3. Items that distinguished between men and women were dropped so that direct comparison could be made between the orientations of these two groups. (Differences in orientation between men and women in any case were not marked.)

After all decisions have been made about what should constitute "work orientations" and what items should be chosen to measure the concepts, there is still the question, Are the scales adequate? The following criteria and discussion are offered as bases for an answer.

1. The items constituting each scale should be meaningful. As indicated in Chapter 2, the scales are made up of elements which yield work orientations that have psychological and behavioral significance.

2. Each scale should have a sufficiently high reliability coefficient—at least 0.50. The coefficients reported in Table B-1 for the nine orientations range from 0.60 to 0.88.

3. The average intercorrelations among items belonging to the same scale should be higher than the average intercorrelations between these items and those of any other scale, and indeed, Table B-1 shows this.

4. The work orientation scales should fulfill the first three criteria for both poor and nonpoor persons. Table B-1 presents the data for four groups of respondents: welfare males, nonwelfare males, nonwelfare females, and welfare females. The three criteria apply to each group separately, indicating the legitimacy of comparing the work orientation scores of poor and nonpoor persons.

This discussion and the data in Table B-1 indicate that the nine orientations discussed in the main text are reasonably reliable, distinct, and psychologically significant measures of orientations toward work of both the poor and the relatively affluent.

Orientations and Items Omitted from the Main Text

To conserve space, not all the orientations measured in this study were mentioned in the main text. One of them consists of items that were rated on the ladder measuring best–worst way of life. These items were phrased as opposites to those constituting the life aspirations orientation. Thus, while "good health" constitutes an item in the life aspirations orientation, "poor health" constitutes an item in the negative life aspirations orientation. This orientation is important and reliable. Both poor and nonpoor persons give it low scores, rejecting such things as "poor health." The scores correlate negatively with scores on life aspirations and work ethic but positively with acceptability of quasi-illegal activities. In short, responses to the negative life aspirations orientation are entirely reasonable but do not contribute much beyond what is revealed by other orientations. Hence it was ignored in the main discussion.

The same argument applies to the omission of an orientation that appears only for males and is called work as a means to positive relations with others. This scale consists of the following five occupational goal items rated on an agree–disagree ladder.

To me, a very important part of work is the opportunity to make friends.

The main satisfaction a person can get out of work is helping other people.

It is more important for a job to have the respect of family and friends than to provide a lot of money.

It's important for me to have a job where there is a lot of responsibility.

It's important for me to have a job that makes my community a better place to live in.

These items appear as part of the work ethic orientation for females but cluster as a separate scale for males. To make the scales comparable for men and women, these items have been eliminated from the work ethic measurement for women. The scale measuring work as a means to positive relations with others shows a strong positive correlation with work ethic. Little new information on mean scores and correlations with other orientations is provided by the scale beyond that already available in the work ethic measurement for men. Hence the orientation for positive relations with others has not been analyzed in the main text.

TABLE B-1. Reliability of Work Orientations and Mean Values of Correlations among Items

Orientation[a]	Reliability coefficient[b]	Life aspirations	Work ethic	Lack of confidence	Acceptability of quasi-illegal activities	Acceptability of welfare	Work beyond need for money	Train to improve earning ability	Job discrimination	Work if on welfare
Life aspirations (14)										
Welfare males[c]	0.88	0.34[d]	0.14	0.03	−0.18	0.01	0.08	0.22	0.01	...
Nonwelfare males[e]	0.71	0.13	0.08	0.03	−0.05	0.00	0.03	0.07	0.00	...
Nonwelfare females[f]	0.66	0.12	0.06	0.04	−0.04	0.02	0.03	0.08	0.02	0.03
Welfare females[g]	0.80	0.22	0.06	0.04	−0.05	0.01	0.05	0.10	0.04	0.05
Work ethic (15)										
Welfare males	0.81	0.14	0.22	0.06	−0.13	0.02	0.10	0.14	0.06	...
Nonwelfare males	0.73	0.08	0.15	0.09	−0.04	0.01	0.09	0.06	−0.04	...
Nonwelfare females	0.71	0.06	0.14	0.07	−0.04	0.02	0.07	0.07	0.01	0.04
Welfare females	0.75	0.06	0.17	0.06	−0.05	0.00	0.07	0.10	0.07	0.10
Lack of confidence (8)										
Welfare males	0.73	0.03	0.06	0.25	0.02	0.11	0.01	0.04	0.12	...
Nonwelfare males	0.71	0.03	0.02	0.24	0.05	0.09	0.02	0.04	0.02	...
Nonwelfare females	0.70	0.04	0.07	0.23	0.01	0.11	0.02	0.06	0.04	0.02
Welfare females	0.73	0.04	0.06	0.25	0.01	0.13	0.02	0.03	0.11	0.01
Acceptability of quasi-illegal activities (8)										
Welfare males	0.74	−0.18	−0.13	0.02	0.27	0.02	−0.09	−0.21	0.00	...
Nonwelfare males	0.62	−0.05	−0.04	0.05	0.17	0.06	−0.02	−0.05	0.00	...
Nonwelfare females	0.60	−0.04	−0.04	0.01	0.16	0.05	−0.02	−0.04	0.00	−0.02
Welfare females	0.62	−0.05	−0.05	0.01	0.17	0.02	−0.03	−0.10	−0.01	−0.02
Acceptability of welfare (5)										
Welfare males	0.61	0.01	0.02	0.11	0.02	0.24	0.02	−0.02	0.08	...
Nonwelfare males	0.65	0.00	0.01	0.09	0.06	0.27	0.04	0.05	0.10	...
Nonwelfare females	0.68	0.02	0.02	0.11	0.05	0.30	0.03	0.07	0.08	0.08
Welfare females	0.67	0.01	0.00	0.13	0.02	0.29	0.03	0.01	0.06	0.00

Work beyond need for money (4)

Welfare males	0.70	0.08	0.19	0.01	−0.09	0.02	[0.37]	0.13	0.07	...
Nonwelfare males	0.74	0.03	0.09	0.02	−0.02	0.04	[0.42]	0.03	−0.03	...
Nonwelfare females	0.73	0.03	0.07	0.02	−0.02	0.03	[0.40]	0.04	−0.01	0.03
Welfare females	0.65	0.05	0.07	0.02	−0.03	0.03	[0.32]	0.09	0.01	0.08

Train to improve earning ability (4)

Welfare males	0.79	0.22	0.14	0.04	−0.21	−0.02	0.13	[0.48]	0.04	...
Nonwelfare males	0.81	0.07	0.06	0.04	−0.05	0.05	0.03	[0.51]	0.03	...
Nonwelfare females	0.76	0.08	0.06	0.06	−0.04	0.07	0.04	[0.45]	0.07	0.13
Welfare females	0.70	0.10	0.10	0.03	−0.10	0.10	0.09	[0.37]	0.04	0.15

Job discrimination (2)

Welfare males	0.60	0.01	0.06	0.12	0.00	0.08	0.07	0.04	[0.43]	...
Nonwelfare males	0.75	0.00	−0.04	0.02	0.00	0.10	−0.03	0.03	[0.63]	...
Nonwelfare females	0.76	0.02	0.01	0.04	0.00	0.08	−0.01	0.07	[0.61]	0.03
Welfare females	0.64	0.04	0.07	0.11	−0.01	0.06	0.01	0.04	[0.47]	0.02

Work if on welfare (5)

Welfare males	...	...	...	...	...	...	...	...	...	...
Nonwelfare males	...	...	...	...	...	...	...	...	...	...
Nonwelfare females	0.79	0.03	0.04	0.02	−0.02	0.03	0.03	0.13	0.03	[0.43]
Welfare females	0.75	0.05	0.10	0.01	−0.02	0.08	0.08	0.15	0.02	[0.37]

a. The number of items making up the orientation are shown in parentheses.

b. Reliability estimates are based on the average correlation among items in the scale and the number of items, according to the well-known psychometric formula:

$$\text{Reliability} = \frac{(\text{number of items})(\text{average intercorrelation})}{1 + (\text{numbers of items} - 1)(\text{average intercorrelation})}.$$

For a discussion of reliability and this formula, see Jum Nunnally, *Psychometric Theory* (McGraw-Hill, 1967), p. 193.

c. There were 644 welfare males: 255 from WIN and 389 sons of long- and short-term Baltimore welfare mothers.

d. The figures in brackets are the average correlations between the items that make up the *same* orientation. All other figures are the average correlations between items of *different* orientations.

e. There were 1,015 nonwelfare males: 740 outer-city black fathers and sons and 275 outer-city white fathers and sons.

f. There were 998 nonwelfare females: 748 outer-city black mothers and daughters and 250 outer-city white mothers and daughters.

g. There were 1,315 welfare females: 926 from WIN and 389 long- and short-term Baltimore welfare mothers.

A third scale that was eliminated because it did not appear to provide new information was called "desirability of fame and job respect." It is composed in part of two life goals, rated on the ladder designated best–worst way of life: "owning an expensive car" and "being famous." Three income beliefs make up the rest of the scale: "having a job that your friends respect," "having a job where you direct a lot of other people," and "having a job where you could become famous."

A fourth scale was rejected for further analysis because it had low reliability (less than 0.6), appeared only for men, and provided little new information. It is called "dirty work" and consists of five income beliefs, rated on the ladder labeled best–worst way of getting enough to live on.

Having a job that pays a lot of money but there is a lot of hard physical work.

Having a job where you earn a lot of money but the work is very dirty.

Having a job that pays a lot of money but you will be fired if you don't work hard.

Having a job with dirty working conditions.

Having a job where you are let go when business is slow.

These items look interesting, but apparently contain ambiguities that reduce reliability. The purpose of the scale was to measure willingness to accept menial labor. A broader spectrum of items might yield a reliable scale for men and women.

A few items that also looked appealing but did not cluster with any of the orientations are worth mentioning—the purpose being to indicate that certain attractive-looking concepts are ambiguous.

It is better to be poor than to make a living by breaking the law.

It is more desirable for a mother with small children to stay at home than to go out to work.

Most women who draw welfare prefer to work.

Drawing welfare for a long period of time makes a person feel worthless.

Choosing the Groups to Be Interviewed

As explained in Chapter 2, the welfare mothers and sons were chosen from the Baltimore Department of Welfare's list of recipients of Aid to Families with Dependent Children. More detail on choosing the other groups is given below.

WIN Respondents

The main purpose in interviewing WIN trainees was to determine whether their work orientations at the beginning of the program were related to their work activity at termination from it. The focus was to be on urban rather than rural areas, and southern cities were ruled out because it was felt that they might be slow to implement WIN. Programs in the largest cities, such as New York and Los Angeles, were also avoided because they present special problems and are usually overwhelmed with research efforts. The choice of sites for gathering data on work orientations was narrowed down to moderately large nonsouthern cities having large WIN programs—a total estimated enrollment of around 1,000 trainees.

In recognition of the possibility that geographical differences affect work orientations, it was decided to choose cities in different areas of the country. From a list of twelve possible cities—four each in the East, Midwest, and West—six were chosen on the basis of the willingness of WIN staff to cooperate with the research effort. These sites were the District of Columbia and Baltimore in the East; Detroit and Milwaukee in the Midwest; and Seattle and the San Francisco Bay Area in the West. While they are not necessarily typical of urban WIN sites, wide differences in work orientations by geographical location, if they exist, should be observable in the data they generated. As noted in Appendix C, however, such differences do not exist.

Baltimore Outer-City Black and White Families

The mothers, fathers, and teen-agers interviewed in the outer portions of Baltimore were to serve as a comparison group for the welfare mothers and sons interviewed in the Baltimore ghetto, the purpose being to determine whether the work orientations of poor black mothers and sons were basically different from those of blacks who had made it out of poverty. It was reasoned that black families who had made it would probably be living in racially changing areas of the city, and interviews were carried out in such areas according to the sampling procedure, developed and carried out by Sidney Hollander Associates, described below. White families in these racially changing areas were also interviewed as another comparison group.

The first step in selecting the sample was to list census tracts that satisfied two criteria: (1) at least 25 percent of their 1967 population was estimated to be black (a smaller proportion would make the task of locating eligible black households too difficult); and (2) less than 75 percent of their 1960 population was black (thus increasing the possibility of locating recent movers). This selection was based on the Metropolitan Baltimore Chamber of Commerce, "Negro Market Data Handbook, Metropolitan Baltimore" (November 1968). Twenty-eight such tracts were found. Ten were eliminated because of their inner-city location. Tracts on the fringe between the inner and the outer city were also eliminated unless (according to 1960 Census data) they contained relatively large numbers of single-family, rather than multiunit, structures, since it was hypothesized that families with teen-agers were more likely to be found in houses than in apartments. The original list of twenty-eight "possible" census tracts was thus reduced to fourteen.

The number of black households—the sample universe—included in these fourteen census tracts was then estimated as follows.

1. The total number of housing units in each of the fourteen was assumed to be the same as it was at the time of the 1960 Census, the last date for which precise data are available. This is a reasonable assumption, since all the tracts are within the city limits in areas that were fairly well built up by 1960, so it is unlikely that any appreciable amount of new housing has been added. Nor had any wide-scale demolition taken place.

2. The number of black households in each tract was estimated by multiplying the total number of households by the midpoint of the interval giving the black population percentage in 1967.

This procedure yielded an estimated 21,928 black households in the fourteen census tracts. A skip factor (proportional to the number of households) was then applied to yield fifty sampling areas. Some latitude was used, however, to get a better geographic and economic dispersion of areas; for example, one sampling area was transferred from tract 27-16 to the adjacent 27-17, so that each had three areas instead of there being four in 27-16 and two in 27-17—the statistical distribution.

As shown in Table B-2, most tracts included at least three sampling areas. Boundaries were defined in such a way that areas did not overlap or extend beyond tract boundaries. A starting point was designated for each area—an intersection selected to maximize the inclusion of blocks with higher-than-average value of housing units (as reported in the 1960 Census).

A quota of thirteen interviews was assigned to each sampling area—ten with black households, three with white. In a few instances it was necessary to go beyond tract boundaries to complete the quota of white respondents, since white households within the boundaries did not meet the requirement that they include teen-agers.

TABLE B-2. *Characteristics of Selected Census Tracts, Baltimore, 1960 and 1967*

Census tract	Blacks as a percentage of total population[a]		Number of households, 1960	Estimated percentage of blacks, 1967	Estimated number of black households, 1967	Number of sampling areas
	1960	1967				
28-3	A	B	1,194	37	442	1
28-2	A	C	2,035	62	1,262	3
28-1B	A	B	2,482	37	918	2
27-18	A	B	3,207	37	1,187	3
27-17	A	B	2,079	37	769	3
27-16	A	D	1,979	87	1,722	3
27-10	B	D	2,659	87	2,313	5
20-7	C	D	2,604	87	2,265	5
20-6	B	C	1,342	62	832	2
16-8	A	D	2,883	87	2,508	7
15-3	A	D	1,910	87	1,662	4
15-12	A	D	2,011	87	1,750	3
15-11	B	D	2,691	87	2,341	5
15-10	A	D	2,249	87	1,957	4
Total	...	...	31,325	...	21,928	50

a. A: Less than 25 percent. B: 25 to 49 percent. C: 50 to 74 percent. D: 75 percent or more.

Appendix C

Additional Data

Rank Order of All Life Goals for Mothers and Fathers

To MAKE THE TABLES in the main text less complex, the rank order of only seven of the fourteen goals included in Orientation 1, life aspirations, were given for the welfare and nonwelfare mothers and fathers. The rankings of all fourteen goals are of some interest, however, and they are presented in Tables c-1 and c-2. All groups tend to give high ranking to "good health" and low ranking to "helping other people" and "getting along with your neighbors," indicating that the poor and the nonpoor are alike in placing goals involving themselves above those of helping others.

WIN Responses by Geographical Location

Do respondents from the East and those from the Midwest and West differ in any important respect? Does race make any difference? Table c-3 presents the mean values given eight of the work orientations by WIN trainees from these three geographical regions. The table shows that black female trainees are concentrated in the East, whites in the West.

Only one significant difference by geographical region appears in the work orientation ratings. Black WIN women from the Midwest express less dependence on welfare (Orientation 5) than do other trainees. This finding is difficult to interpret without further data. Perhaps poor midwesterners are more strongly opposed to welfare than the poor in other parts of the country; perhaps there is greater bias in responses to this orientation in Detroit and Milwaukee than in the other cities.

148

TABLE C-1. *Priority Given Life Goals by Welfare and Nonwelfare Mothers*

Rank	Long-term welfare	Short-term welfare	WIN	Outer-city black	Outer-city white
1	Good health	Be honest	Good education	Good health	Good health
2	Good education	Nice place to live	Be honest	Good education	Be honest
3	Husband supports you	Good health	Nice place to live	Husband supports you	Husband supports you
4	Nice place to live	Good education	Good health	Have goals	Good education
5	Good family relations	Husband supports you	Like job	Well-paid job	Good family relations
6	Well-paid job	...	Well-paid job	Be honest	Have goals
6.5	...	Good family relations; Like job	...	...	...
7	Be honest	...	Make better world	Good family relations	Make better world
8	Make better world	Well-paid job	Have goals	Like job	Help others
9	Like job	Have goals	Good family relations	Make better world	Like job
10	Have goals	Help others	Husband supports you	Regular job	Nice place to live
11	Help others	Make better world	Regular job	Help others	Regular job
12	Get along with neighbors	Get along with neighbors	Help others	Get along with neighbors	Well-paid job
13	Regular job	Plenty of money	Get along with neighbors	Plenty of money	Get along with neighbors
14	Plenty of money	Regular job	Plenty of money	Nice place to live	Plenty of money

Number of respondents

267	122	957	500	175

TABLE C-2. *Priority Given Life Goals by Welfare and Nonwelfare Fathers*

Rank	WIN	Outer-city black	Outer-city white
1	Good health	Good health	Good health
2	Good education	Well-paid job	Good family relations
3	Like job	Support family	Be honest
4	...	Good family relations	Support family
4.5	Be honest; Good family relations	...	...
5	...	Good education	Like job
6	Nice place to live	Regular job	Regular job
7	Well-paid job	Like job	Good education
8	Support family	Be honest	Make better world
9	Have goals	Have goals	Have goals
10	Make better world	Make better world	Help others
11	Help others	Plenty of money	Well-paid job
12	Regular job	Get along with neighbors	Nice place to live
13	Get along with neighbors	Help others	Get along with neighbors
14	Plenty of money	Nice place to live	Plenty of money
Number of respondents	244	500	175

The correlations (not presented here) between Orientation 5 and the other orientations for the midwestern group are much like the correlations obtained for the other groups, so the difference in mean ratings is not the product of a basically different view on the part of the midwesterners about the acceptability of welfare. This and the general similarity of means on seven orientations make it appropriate to combine the responses of black WIN trainees across geographical regions.

The lack of significant differences in the mean values of ratings given by white female trainees in the Midwest and West suggests that combining their responses across geographical areas is also appropriate. The same argument applies to male WIN trainees.

Comparability of Nonterminated, Terminated, and Reinterviewed Terminated Black WIN Women

To determine whether there are major differences among the 406 black female trainees who originally completed the work orientation questionnaire in the spring of 1969 but were not terminated by early 1971, the 551 black

TABLE C-3. *Work Orientations of WIN Trainees, by Region, Sex, and Race*
Mean values[a]

Orientation	Black WIN mothers			White WIN mothers[b]		WIN men[c]	
	East[d]	Midwest[e]	West[f]	Midwest[e]	West[f]	East and Midwest	West
1. Life aspirations	3.78	3.69	3.70	3.70	3.68	3.61	3.64
2. Work ethic	3.49	3.39	3.39	3.30	3.40	3.43	3.35
3. Lack of confidence in ability to succeed	2.81	2.62	2.86	2.42	2.56	2.63	2.61
4. Acceptability of quasi-illegal activities	1.15	1.18	1.23	1.26	1.13	1.26	1.35
5. Acceptability of welfare	2.35	2.10[g]	2.47	2.18	2.16	2.18	2.32
6. Work beyond need for money	2.97	2.90	3.11	3.05	3.03	3.00	3.03
7. Train to improve earning ability	3.78	3.67	3.65	3.61	3.71	3.68	3.61
8. Job discrimination	2.93	2.80	2.96	2.25	2.54	2.68	2.61
Number of respondents	567	229	161	59	169	89	165

a. All items in each orientation are rated on a four-point scale. The higher the rating, the more strongly the orientation is held.
b. There was only one white WIN female respondent in the East; her responses were included with those from the Midwest.
c. Not broken down by race because there would be too few cases. The ten teen-agers are included.
d. District of Columbia and Baltimore.
e. Detroit and Milwaukee.
f. Seattle and the San Francisco Bay Area.
g. This mean value is substantially different from that of black WIN women in another geographical region.

female trainees who were terminated by early 1971, and the 161 black female terminees who were reinterviewed in the spring of 1971, mean values given to eight orientations by these three groups were compared. They are presented in Table C-4, and show no significant differences.

Table C-5 sets forth the geographical distribution of all the WIN women —which includes the terminated and nonterminated trainees and those reinterviewed. Most of the reinterviewing was done in the East, where the concentration of black women is highest, because there were fewer terminations in the Midwest and West and because of budget limitations. Results reported in Chapter 7 about the relation of work orientations to work activity may possibly be applicable only to black WIN women in the East. On the other hand, the data presented in the previous section suggest that black women in the Midwest and West are not much different from those in the East. Results obtained from the eastern group are therefore likely to be valid for all.

TABLE C-4. *Mean Values on Orientations at Time of Entry into WIN for Black WIN Women at Later Stages*

Orientation or characteristic	Still in WIN	Terminated from WIN	Terminated and reinterviewed[a]
1. Life aspirations	3.74	3.75	3.77
2. Work ethic	3.45	3.45	3.47
3. Lack of confidence in ability to succeed	2.79	2.76	2.75
4. Acceptability of quasi-illegal activities	1.16	1.17	1.17
5. Acceptability of welfare	2.35	2.28	2.26
6. Work beyond need for money	3.07	2.90	2.86
7. Train to improve earning ability	3.72	3.74	3.75
8. Job discrimination	2.86	2.94	2.98
Number of respondents	406	551	161
Age	30	29	29
Education (years)	10	10	10

a. The number of black women reinterviewed was 188, but 27 had mixed work and nonwork experience between time of termination and time of reinterview and were dropped from the analysis in Chapter 7.

Average Ratings and Correlations of Welfare and Nonwelfare Respondents

In Chapter 6 comparisons were made of the median values of certain means and correlations given by the welfare and nonwelfare respondents, who were grouped into five units. Tables C-6 and C-7 set forth the means and correlations for the subgroups of each unit, from which the medians were calculated.

TABLE C-5. *Geographical Distribution of Black WIN Women*

Location	All		Terminated		Reinterviewed		
	Number	*Percentage of total*	*Number*	*Percentage of total*	*Number*	*Percentage of total*	*Percentage of terminees reinterviewed*
District of Columbia	347	36	293	53	133	71	45
Baltimore	220	23	103	19	27	14	26
Detroit	166	17	60	11	13	7	21
Milwaukee[a]	63	7	34	6	...	...	...
Seattle[a]	24	3	16	3	...	...	...
San Francisco Bay Area	137	14	45	8	15	8	33
Total	957	100	551	100	188	100	34

a. Reinterviewing not undertaken because of budget limitations.

TABLE c-6. *Mean Values Given Selected Work Orientations by Five Units of Respondents*

| | | | | *Orientation* | | |
| | | | | *Acceptability* | | |
Unit and components	*Life aspirations*	*Work ethic*	*Lack of confidence*	*of quasi-illegal activities*	*Acceptability of welfare*	*Job discrimination*
Unit 1						
Long-term welfare: 267 mothers	3.66	3.21	3.13	1.26	2.92	2.81
267 sons	3.56	3.40	2.99	1.35	2.38	3.08
Short-term welfare: 122 mothers	3.71	3.28	3.13	1.16	2.88	3.15
122 sons	3.65	3.37	3.12	1.27	2.44	3.19
Unit 2						
Black WIN trainees: 81 men	3.61	3.40	2.76	1.33	2.40	2.84
957 women	3.75	3.45	2.77	1.17	2.31	2.91
Unit 3						
White WIN trainees: 163 men	3.63	3.36	2.55	1.32	2.21	2.52
228 women	3.69	3.37	2.52	1.17	2.16	2.47
Unit 4						
Outer-city blacks: 500 mothers	3.75	3.43	3.19	1.12	2.12	2.68
500 fathers	3.71	3.53	3.22	1.34	1.97	2.72
250 sons	3.66	3.41	3.14	1.26	1.97	2.48
250 daughters	3.72	3.36	3.08	1.19	2.19	2.47
Unit 5						
Outer-city whites: 175 mothers	3.71	3.34	2.61	1.04	1.53	2.05
175 fathers	3.66	3.41	2.44	1.15	1.61	2.15
100 sons	3.58	3.16	2.49	1.26	1.69	2.28
75 daughters	3.58	3.13	2.32	1.23	1.58	2.21

TABLE C-7. *Correlations between Selected Work Orientations and Characteristics for Five Units of Respondents*

| | Orientation or characteristic | | |
	Work ethic	Acceptability of welfare	Level of education
Orientation and unit			
Lack of confidence			
Unit 1: Welfare			
Long-term: 267 mothers	0.26	0.23	−0.17
267 sons	0.17	0.29	−0.15
Short-term: 122 mothers	0.32	0.05	−0.23
122 sons	0.41	0.32	−0.23
Unit 2: Black WIN trainees			
81 men	0.25	0.32	−0.29
957 women	0.22	0.31	−0.14
Unit 3: White WIN trainees			
163 men	0.12	0.38	−0.29
228 women	0.24	0.22	−0.20
Unit 4: Outer-city blacks			
500 mothers	0.26	0.25	−0.23
500 fathers	0.33	0.27	−0.36
250 sons	0.26	0.18	−0.01
250 daughters	0.31	0.17	−0.13
Unit 5: Outer-city whites			
175 mothers	0.08	0.01	−0.34
175 fathers	0.16	0.23	−0.26
100 sons	0.29	0.10	−0.13
75 daughters	0.14	0.11	−0.13
Acceptability of welfare			
Unit 1: Welfare			
Long-term: 267 mothers	...	...	−0.15
267 sons	...	...	−0.23
Short-term: 122 mothers	...	...	−0.24
122 sons	...	...	−0.21
Unit 2: Black WIN trainees			
81 men	...	...	−0.33
957 women	...	...	−0.16
Unit 3: White WIN trainees			
163 men	...	...	−0.23
228 women	...	...	−0.14
Unit 4: Outer-city blacks			
500 mothers	...	...	−0.19
500 fathers	...	...	−0.17
250 sons	...	...	−0.06
250 daughters	...	...	−0.27
Unit 5: Outer-city whites			
175 mothers	...	...	−0.21
175 fathers	...	...	−0.08
100 sons	...	...	0.07
75 daughters	...	...	−0.10

Notes

1. Many statements have been made about the importance of work. Three are offered here by way of illustration. "Thus a man's work is one of the things by which he is judged, and certainly one of the more significant things by which he judges himself. . . . A man's work is one of the more important parts of his social identity, of his self; indeed, of his fate in the one life he has to live." Everett C. Hughes, *Men and Their Work* (Free Press, 1958), pp. 42–43.

"In my own studies bearing on the meaning of work for the individual . . . I was helped by an almost casual remark Freud made in a footnote in *Civilization and Its Discontents*. . . . He said that work is man's strongest tie to reality. . . . I shall begin by turning Freud's statement around: that is, if work is man's strongest tie to reality, then the absence of work should leave him less solidly in touch with reality. This is indeed the case, as several studies of unemployment have demonstrated. . . . Work encourages the continuous action necessary to maintain objective knowledge of reality; work permits the pleasurable experience of competence; work adds to the store of conventional knowledge." Marie Jahoda, "Notes on Work," in Rudolph Lowenstein and others (eds.), *Psychoanalysis: A General Psychology* (New York: International Universities Press, 1966), pp. 623–28.

"Our society as a whole will benefit when welfare recipients become taxpayers, and new jobholders increase the Nation's buying power. These are dollars and cents advantages. But there is no way to estimate the value of a decent job that replaces hostility and anger with hope and opportunity. There is no way to estimate the respect of a boy or girl for his parent who has earned a place in our world. There is no way to estimate the stirring of the American dream of learning, saving, and building a life of independence." Lyndon B. Johnson, message "To the Congress of the United States," January 23, 1968, in *Manpower Report of the President* (April 1968), p. xv.

2. A study of unemployment resulting from the depression of the 1930s found that persons who were paid for working on public work projects had more self-respect than those who received relief payments without doing any work. E. Wight Bakke, *The Unemployed Worker: A Study of the Task of Making a Living Without a Job* (Yale University Press for the Institute of Human Relations, 1940), pp. 420–25.

3. A Labor Department report computes a "subemployment" index, rather than an unemployment index, which counts not only persons who are unemployed and looking for work, but also those who can obtain only part-time work when they want full-time work and heads of households who earn less than $56 a week. The average subemployment index for ten metropolitan areas surveyed in 1966 is given as 33.9 percent. W. Willard Wirtz, *A Sharper Look at Unemployment in U.S. Cities and Slums: A Summary Report Submitted to The President by The Secretary of Labor* (U.S. Department of Labor, no date).

4. In 1959, there were only 0.8 million families in the United States receiving Aid to Families with Dependent Children. By 1965, the figure had risen to 1.1 million, and by 1971, to 2.7 million. See U.S. Department of Health, Education, and Welfare, Welfare Administration, *Welfare in Review, Statistical Supplement 1966 Edition*, Table 3; and HEW, Social and Rehabilitation Service, *Public Assistance Statistics, June 1971*, p. 8, Table 1.

5. Two main proponents of the "culture of poverty" are Oscar Lewis, who has studied poor families in Mexico, Puerto Rico, and New York City, and Walter B. Miller, who has studied white teen-age gangs in the Boston area. Oscar Lewis, *La Vida* (Random House, 1965), pp. xliv–lii; Walter B. Miller, "Lower Class Culture as a Generating Milieu of Gang Delinquency," *Journal of Social Issues*, Vol. 14 (July 1958), pp. 5–19.

6. Lola M. Irelan, Oliver C. Moles, and Robert M. O'Shea, in "Ethnicity, Poverty, and Selected Attitudes: A Test of the 'Culture of Poverty' Hypothesis" (*Social Forces*, Vol. 47 [June 1969], pp. 405–13), point out that, while Oscar Lewis has not made work a focus of the divergency between the "culture of poverty" and the larger culture, it is reasonable to infer from his position that the poor dislike work.

7. For a discussion of the limitations of the "culture of poverty" thesis and a presentation of alternative views, see Jack L. Roach and Orville R. Gursslin, "An Evaluation of the Concept 'Culture of Poverty,'" *Social Forces*, Vol. 45 (March 1967), pp. 383–92.

8. The major journals for reporting studies about the attitudes and performance of employed workers are the *Journal of Applied Psychology* and *Personnel Psychology*. For a useful discussion of various theories and findings about work motivation and performance, see Victor H. Vroom, *Work and Motivation* (Wiley, 1964).

9. Walter S. Neff, *Work and Human Behavior* (Atherton, 1968), p. 247.

10. William L. Yancey, "Intervention Research: A Strategy of Social Inquiry" (paper presented at the 1965 meeting of the American Sociological Association; processed).

11. Lee Rainwater, *Behind Ghetto Walls* (Aldine, 1970), p. 176.

12. Elliot Liebow, *Tally's Corner: A Study of Negro Streetcorner Men* (Little, Brown, 1967), pp. 29–71.

13. Walter B. Miller, "White Gangs," *Transaction*, Vol. 6 (September 1969), pp. 11–26.

14. Irelan, Moles, and O'Shea, "Ethnicity, Poverty, and Selected Attitudes."

15. Leonard Reissman, "Readiness to Succeed: Mobility Aspirations and Modernism Among the Poor," *Urban Affairs Quarterly*, Vol. 4 (March 1969), pp. 379–95. There is some question whether averaging together responses to ten items, as done in the above study, is useful. Reissman refers to an earlier study of the scalability of these items, which, using a factor analysis of the same ten items, reveals three factors with only two or three items on each factor having a loading greater than thirty. See John E. Dunkelberger, "Measures of Job Mobility or Financial Aspiration," in Charles L. Cleland (ed.), *Scaling Social Data*, Southern Cooperative Series Bulletin 108 (December 1965), pp. 38–39.

16. Lawrence Podell, "Families on Welfare in New York City" (City University of New York, Bernard M. Baruch College, Graduate Division, Center for the Study of Urban Problems, 1968; processed), p. 17.

17. Perry Levinson, "How Employable Are AFDC Women?" *Welfare in Review*, Vol. 8 (July–August 1970), p. 16.

18. David Gottlieb, "Poor Youth Do Want to Be Middle Class But It's Not Easy," *Personnel and Guidance Journal*, Vol. 46 (October 1967), pp. 116–22.

19. "Codebook: Mobilization for Youth," Vol. 4: "Intergenerational Comparisons, Decks 1–3" (Columbia University, New York School of Social Work, Research Center, 1962; processed), pp. 28–32.

20. "Study of the Meaning, Experience, and Effects of the Neighborhood Youth Corps on Negro Youth Who Are Seeking Work" (New York University, Graduate School of Social Work, Center for the Study of Unemployed Youth, 1967; processed), Pt. 1, pp. 144–65.

21. Harold L. Sheppard and A. Harvey Belitsky, *The Job Hunt: Job-Seeking Behavior of Unemployed Workers in a Local Economy* (Johns Hopkins Press, 1966). In analyzing the relation between achievement motivation and reemployment, the authors eliminate certain of their cases after the data have been collected in order to present "significant" results. "If we eliminate skilled workers from the analysis and also eliminate Negroes (since their job-finding chances are low, regardless of motivation), the relationship between re-employment and achievement motivation among white semi-skilled and unskilled workers is more definite" (p. 115). This seems a dubious procedure.

22. Bernard P. Indik, "The Motivation To Work" (New Brunswick: Rutgers University, Institute of Management and Labor Relations, Research Program, 1966; processed), p. 73.

23. Frank Friedlander and Stuart Greenberg, "Effect of Job Attitudes, Training, and Organization Climate on Performance of the Hard-Core Unemployed," *Journal of Applied Psychology*, Vol. 55 (August 1971), pp. 287–95.

24. Gerald Gurin, "Inner-City Negro Youth in a Job Training Project: A Study of Factors Related to Attrition and Job Success," U.S. Department of Labor, Manpower Administration, MDTA Experimental and Demonstration Findings No. 7 (1968; processed), pp. 98–113.

25. The relationship of measurement of psychological attributes to overt activity has long been an issue in social-psychological research. See, for example, Howard J. Ehrlich, "Attitudes, Behavior, and the Intervening Variables"; Irwin Deutscher, "Looking Backward: Case Studies on the Progress of Methodology in Sociological Research"; and Richard T. LaPiere, "Comment on Irwin Deutscher's Looking Backward," *American Sociologist*, Vol. 4 (February 1969), pp. 29–34, 35–41, and 41–42, respectively. See also "Letters," *American Sociologist*, Vol. 4 (August 1969), pp. 249–51.

26. For a more extended discussion of this feedback action model, see Leonard Goodwin, "Conceptualizing the Action Process: How the Actions of Individuals Relate to the Guiding of Social Change," *Sociology and Social Research*, Vol. 50 (April 1966), pp. 377–92.

27. These have on occasion been given different titles by different authors. For example, it is not unusual for the term "attitude" to incorporate three of the elements introduced in this study. As one specialist in attitude measurement points out, "Discussions of social attitudes usually focus on three classes of phenomena. One of these is cognitive in nature and refers to an individual's information regarding an issue [belief, in our terms]. Another is behavioral, referring to the acts which an individual performs,

advocates, or facilitates with regard to an issue [intention, in our terms]. The third phenomenon is affective, referring to the individual's valuations [attitude, in our terms]." Harry S. Upshaw, "Attitude Measurement," in Hubert M. Blalock, Jr., and Ann B. Blalock (eds.), *Methodology in Social Research* (McGraw-Hill, 1968), p. 60.

The position taken in this study is that "attitude" should be regarded only as the affective reaction toward work, with separate measures being created for belief and intention regarding work. Martin Fishbein uses the term "attitude" this way in "Attitude and the Prediction of Behavior," in Fishbein (ed.), *Readings in Attitude Theory and Measurement* (Wiley, 1967), pp. 477–92. Milton Rokeach, on the other hand, gives the term "belief" cognitive, conative, and affective dimensions and then defines an "attitude" as a constellation of beliefs. *Beliefs, Attitudes, and Values: A Theory of Organization and Change* (San Francisco: Jossey-Bass, 1968), pp. 112–14.

Beyond the somewhat arbitrary matter of terminology, the psychological elements presented in this paper are in general use in the psychological and sociological fields. (The concept of "goal," another of our psychological elements, is also common in these fields, though often it is not explicitly differentiated in attitude measurement as such.) The approach of this study is to define the goals, beliefs, attitude, and intentions relating to work as separate elements, and to obtain empirical measures of these elements, which are then allowed to combine with one another in the empirical analysis to form what are here called "orientations" (somewhat in the way chemical elements might combine to form compounds). The proposal made in this study is that these psychological "compounds," or orientations, be regarded as directly influencing work activities.

CHAPTER 2

1. The author wishes to express his appreciation to Edgar F. Borgatta of the University of Wisconsin for his advice on the use of factor analysis as a clustering technique. The author, of course, assumes full responsibility for the results and interpretations presented here.

2. To the extent that Orientation 3 includes items suggesting that success is a matter of luck and knowing the right people, it would appear at first glance to be measuring the same attributes as the "internal-external" scale developed by Julian B. Rotter. See "Generalized Expectancies for Internal versus External Control of Reinforcement," *Psychological Monographs: General and Applied*, Vol. 80, No. 1 (Washington: American Psychological Association, 1966).

The technique Rotter used, however, is the "forced choice" of items.

For example, a respondent is asked to agree with only one of the following:

11.a. Becoming a success is a matter of hard work, luck has little or nothing to do with it.

b. Getting a good job depends mainly on being in the right place at the right time. (p. 11)

For each item referring to external control that is checked, the respondent is given a score of 1. Total score is the sum of the scores for each item. The variable being measured is not "internal control" or "external control" as such, but the extent to which "external control" is chosen over "internal control."

Our lack of confidence orientation, on the other hand, taps only the variable of "external control" and so is not directly comparable to Rotter's scale. His scale has the disadvantage of automatically eliminating any examination of the relation between internal and external control. In this study, a positive relation appears between these two variables (to the extent that lack of confidence measures external control and work ethic measures internal control). This is a finding of some significance and shows the advantage of measuring the two variables separately. The positive relation between the two presumably different variables may be a reason for the modest reliability Rotter obtains for his "I-E" scale of twenty-three items: around 0.70 (p. 13).

3. To avoid the possible introduction of bias, the mothers were told that their names had been chosen from a sample, but its source was not revealed. Thus no respondent would fear her answers might jeopardize her welfare status (nor were responses seen by any member of the welfare department).

4. This racial imbalance is a function of geography. The welfare population of inner cities in the Northeast are mostly black. If it had been feasible to interview welfare families in western cities such as Seattle or San Francisco, a substantial number of white welfare families would have been included.

5. The results of attempting to interview 356 long-term welfare mothers and sons are:

	Percent
Completed pairs	75.4
Moved	9.8
Refused	7.0
Unavailable	5.3
Only one of the pair interviewed	2.5
	100.0

6. The results of attempting to interview 179 short-term mothers and sons are:

	Percent
Completed pairs	68.1
Moved	14.0
Refused	9.5
Unavailable	7.8
Only one of the pair interviewed	0.6
	100.0

7. WIN was created in 1967 by amendments to the Social Security Act. The legislation calls for "appropriate" welfare recipients to participate in WIN or face the loss of welfare payments. Priorities for participation placed welfare fathers in the first category. The second and third categories included teen-age children of welfare parents who were not in school and welfare mothers with no preschool children. For a detailed presentation of program requirements, see U.S. Department of Labor, Manpower Administration, "Work Incentive Program Handbook" (1968; processed).

8. The general procedure for administering the questionnaire involved instruction from the project director to staff members, who then met with trainees during one of the orientation or initial basic education sessions. With a questionnaire in front of him as the staff member read the directions and items aloud, each trainee recorded his ratings; he placed his completed questionnaire in a sealed envelope addressed to the project director and mailed it at the WIN office. Since they knew the questionnaire would go directly to the project director and that WIN staff members would not see them, trainees were under no compulsion to complete the questionnaire or to put their name on it. (Names were necessary for analyzing correlations between work orientations and work activity and for reinterviews; see Chapter 7.) Virtually all WIN trainees who attended on the days the questionnaire was administered completed it, and of the forms returned, fewer than 1 percent were blank or otherwise unusable, and only about 1 percent of the usable questionnaires had no name. On the average, only about 70 percent of those expected on a given day actually appeared; however, those in attendance can reasonably be regarded as typical of participants in these programs.

9. Carol H. Weiss, "Validity of Interview Responses of Welfare Mothers: Final Report," submitted to the Social and Rehabilitation Service, Department of Health, Education, and Welfare (New York: Columbia University, Bureau of Applied Social Research, 1968; processed), pp. 71–74.

10. One might think of using other behavior, such as specific actions, to measure the veracity of expressed psychological orientations. There seems little reason, however, to assume a clear and unambiguous relation between verbal statements and actions. Indeed, this study is concerned with determining the relation between psychological orientations and overt actions.

11. J. Allen Williams, Jr., "Interviewer-Respondent Interaction: A Study of Bias in the Information Interview," *Sociometry*, Vol. 27 (September 1964), pp. 338–52.

12. Barbara Snell Dohrenwend, John Colombotos, and Bruce P. Dohrenwend, "Social Distance and Interviewer Effects," *Public Opinion Quarterly*, Vol. 22 (Fall 1968), pp. 410–22. It has been known for some time that racial differences between interviewer and interviewee may cause bias in responses. See, for example, Howard Schuman and Jean M. Converse, "The Effects of Black and White Interviewers on Black Responses in 1968," *Public Opinion Quarterly*, Vol. 35 (Spring 1971), pp. 44–68. The way class status of interviewer affects response bias has not been thoroughly explored.

13. Weiss, "Validity of Interview Responses of Welfare Mothers."

14. It should be emphasized that this was not designed as a methodological study of the effect of various interviewer characteristics on interviewee responses. The characteristics of race, class, and sex are not adequately represented among the twenty interviewers for such a determination. For example, there are no white lower-class interviewers in the group. The mixture used nevertheless showed that certain interviewer characteristics do affect the ratings of certain work orientations. The results permit a more realistic interpretation and adjustment of certain mean values while indicating the lack of bias in ratings given to other orientations.

15. To show that the correlations between interviewer characteristics and responses on orientations were not the result of certain interviewers being assigned to an unusual sample of respondents, in each case where interviewers' characteristics were reported to be highly associated with orientation scores (a correlation greater than 0.20), a check was made to see whether they had been assigned a representative group of respondents. Correlations were calculated between interviewer characteristics and the age and education of respondents. In all cases these correlations were virtually zero, indicating that interviewers were gathering information from respondents having the same characteristics, at least in the important matters of age and education.

16. As pointed out in the response-bias study in North Carolina (see note 11), there are also theoretical reasons to believe that the responses of blacks to other blacks about certain items are likely to represent "truer" views than responses given by blacks to white interviewers.

17. For discussions of the use and limitation of significance levels, see Denton E. Morrison and Ramon E. Henkel, "Significance Tests Reconsidered," and Robert F. Winch and Donald T. Campbell, "Proof? No. Evidence? Yes. The Significance of Tests of Significance," *American Sociologist*, Vol. 4 (May 1969), pp. 131-40 and 140-43, respectively.

CHAPTER 3

1. Women on welfare at the time of interview could not earn much money without losing their welfare status. Nevertheless, the kinds of jobs they had reflected the general level of their education and skill, and probably had little to do with whether or not they were on welfare.

2. The mean rating given Orientation 2 by ninety long-term welfare mothers when interviewers were high-status whites was 3.69, substantially higher than the mean of 3.21 given by seventy-five mothers to low-status black interviewers. Since the higher figure probably represents respondents' attempts to impress white interviewers with a positive work orientation, it is not included in Table 3-2. The lower rating of 3.21 is not significantly different from the ratings of other groups. (Short-term welfare mothers were interviewed by blacks only so there was no need to control for race.) WIN women completed the questionnaire on their own; thus there was no chance to check for this kind of bias. While their slightly higher rating may reflect some bias toward pleasing middle-class persons, their rating's similarity to the adjusted rating of the long- and short-term welfare mothers argues for its validity.

3. A number of studies have shown that higher-level workers are more concerned about "intrinsic" or self-development goals in their work while lower-level workers are more concerned with "extrinsic" goals, such as the physical conditions under which they work. Two such studies are Richard Centers and Daphne E. Bugental, "Intrinsic and Extrinsic Job Motivations Among Different Segments of the Working Population," *Journal of Applied Psychology*, Vol. 50 (June 1966), pp. 193-97; and Frank Friedlander, "Comparative Work Value Systems," *Personnel Psychology*, Vol. 18 (Spring 1965), pp. 1-20. The Centers and Bugental effort involved interviews with 692 employed men and women, representing a cross-section of greater Los Angeles. The authors point out that respondents were asked, "Which of these things is most important in keeping you on your present job?" Workers are therefore responding to the conditions of their present job rather than to what they would most like in a job. Similarly, in Friedlander's study, 1,500 government employees in an isolated community were asked to rate their satisfaction or dissatisfaction with various attributes of their work

environment and then were asked to rate "the relative importance of these environmental factors." In both studies the workers in occupations of higher prestige were more concerned with intrinsic rewards and the lower level workers with extrinsic rewards. A limitation in both these studies is the lack of distinction between a worker's concrete experience on a job and the goals he might hold about work outside that framework.

The author analyzed the responses of a national sample of American workers to certain open-ended questions and rating items about work; see Leonard Goodwin, "Occupational Goals and Satisfactions of the American Work Force," *Personnel Psychology*, Vol. 22 (Autumn 1969), pp. 313–25. Later, he carried out a further analysis of the items that had been rated on the "agree–disagree" ladder by the national sample of employed workers. Separate factor analyses were completed for the 252 workers who had some college education, the 476 high-school-graduate workers, and the 299 workers who did not complete high school.

For each of the educational groups there emerged a factor containing five of the items included in the work ethic orientation of this study. These common items included: "Getting recognition for my own work is important to me," and "To me, it's important to have the kind of work that gives me a chance to develop my own special abilities." There are no significant differences in mean values given to these five items by the three sets of workers with different educational levels. Hence, when the issue is posed outside the context of their immediate job experience, the goal of finding self-development in work is held as strongly by low-level as by high-level workers in the national sample.

4. This interpretation is supported by the findings of a study by Johnette B. Clark, Stanley Lichtenstein, and Paul Spector, "Social Requirements of Successful Work" (Washington: American Institutes for Research, 1969; processed). The study compared interview responses of 140 men and women in Job Corps training programs with responses of persons already employed in positions for which the Job Corps members were being trained (clerks and mechanics). The authors conclude: "The trainees appear to feel less secure than incumbents; they are more concerned than incumbents about keeping their jobs and maintaining their good standing with supervisors. . . . Trainees would be highly motivated to do their jobs well, and to get along with their superiors, coworkers, and customers, but they lack confidence in their own abilities" (pp. 52–53).

5. The 283 outer-city black mothers interviewed by middle-class persons gave a mean value of 2.89 to this orientation. When the 217 other mothers were interviewed by lower-class persons, the mean value was 3.19. The latter rating was taken as more valid on the grounds that outer-city blacks

were less willing to admit their concern about money and external forces to middle-class interviewers. Either value is significantly higher than the 2.58 given by outer-city whites, while not significantly different from the 3.13 ratings of the Baltimore welfare mothers.

6. The goal items in Orientation 3 emphasize money as a measure of success. Several studies indicate that lower-class persons give greater emphasis to the so-called extrinsic goal of money and material possessions than to the intrinsic goals of status and education. See F. M. Katz, "The Meaning of Success: Some Differences in Value Systems of Social Classes," *Journal of Social Psychology*, Vol. 62 (1964), pp. 141–48; and Ephraim H. Mizruchi, *Success and Opportunity* (Free Press, 1964), pp. 68–78.

The findings of this study—that the poor rate the lack of confidence orientation (including the individual items referring to money) much higher than do the more affluent—offer some support to this view. However, they provide an insight not given in other studies: that the poor relate the acquisition of money to self-development. External rewards or symbols are for them what status and educational attainment are for the affluent— enhancements of the self. This is shown by the intercorrelations of the responses to a few of the items that make up Orientations 2 (work ethic) and 3, as given by 389 long-term and short-term welfare mothers. All correlation coefficients are positive. (The numbers in parentheses are from the questionnaire, Appendix A.)

	Orientation 2 items			
Orientation 3 items	*Importance of recognition* (85)	*Chance to develop abilities* (97)	*Work builds character* (105)	*Success through own efforts* (139)
Success is caring about making money (125)	0.15	0.20	0.14	0.12
Importance of earning good money (132)	0.12	0.19	0.10	0.02
Success is knowing the right people (87)	0.15	0.20	0.13	0.05
Success is a matter of luck (99)	0.13	0.23	0.11	0.01

To merely state that the poor are concerned with material goals and the affluent with self-enhancing goals is to suggest that the poor are unconcerned with self-development. The high mean value given by the poor to the work ethic and the correlations above suggest instead that poor people are as concerned with self-development through work as are more affluent people, but that self-development for the poor involves the attainment of money and material goods to a greater extent than for the nonpoor.

7. The mean values on quasi-illegal activities reported for long- and short-term welfare mothers in Table 3-2 have been adjusted for the class status of the interviewers. The 1.26 rating from seventy-five long-term welfare mothers interviewed by lower-class persons has been used in preference to the 1.14 rating reported to middle-class interviewers; the rating of 1.16 from thirty-seven short-term welfare mothers interviewed by lower-class persons has been used in preference to the 1.06 reported to middle-class interviewers.

8. Depending on government support, however, does not mean liking it. When asked to rate welfare on a four-step ladder ranging from "Best way of getting enough to live on" to "Worst way of getting enough to live on," the average rating of all the welfare women was 1.96. On the other hand, the item about accepting welfare if unable to support oneself or one's family received an average rating of 3.45.

9. It should be mentioned again that the Baltimore welfare mothers knew only that their names had been chosen on a sampling basis. Reference to the welfare list was avoided to decrease the possibility of biasing their responses. No persons from the welfare department had access to any of the raw data.

10. Thomas F. Pettigrew, *A Profile of the Negro American* (Van Nostrand, 1964), p. 51.

11. The interviewers were of course not designated as "higher" or "lower" class to the interviewees. It is assumed that the outer-city black mothers were able to distinguish the high school graduates from the high school dropouts on the basis of subtle differences in dress, language, and behavior. Another possibility is that the interviewers, being themselves biased about these items, were recording the responses of outer-city blacks in a biased fashion. This possibility does not seem too attractive, however, because no such bias occurs when welfare persons are interviewed by higher- and lower-class interviewers.

CHAPTER 4

1. Peter M. Blau and Otis Dudley Duncan, *The American Occupational Structure* (Wiley, 1967), p. 241.

2. Walter B. Miller, "White Gangs," *Transaction*, Vol. 6 (September 1969), pp. 3-26.

3. Leonard Goodwin, "Work Orientations of the Underemployed Poor:

Report on a Pilot Study," *Journal of Human Resources*, Vol. 4 (Fall 1969), pp. 508–19.

4. To establish that a positive correlation between mother-son ratings indicates a flow of influence from mother to son, a longitudinal study indicating how specific mother-son interactions lead to the son's taking on the mother's orientations would be necessary. The lack of this kind of data leaves open the possibility that the similarity of mother-son ratings is the result of some feature in the environment that affects each mother and her son in a particular way but does not involve the transmission of orientations. It is hard to imagine, however, what environmental features would operate in this manner.

5. The lack of a significant correlation very probably indicates no direct parental influence, although it is not impossible that some sons are positively influenced by their parents while others react negatively to their parents' views, yielding in sum a zero correlation.

6. It is important to recognize that even when significant correlations of 0.35 appear between sons' and parents' ratings, most of the variability in sons' ratings is the result of other factors. If one squares a correlation coefficient, the resulting figure indicates the proportion of the total variability in sons' ratings that is accounted for by the mothers' ratings. Thus, if one multiplies 0.35 by itself, the resulting proportion of the variability of welfare sons' ratings accounted for by welfare mothers' ratings is only 0.12. While the mothers are accounting for 12 percent of the variance of sons' scores, 88 percent is accounted for by other factors (which include errors of measurement). Very substantial parental influence is seen when the correlation goes as high as 0.48, as between black outer-city parents and sons. The parents are then accounting for 23 percent of the sons' ratings.

7. There has been considerable speculation on the extent to which the lack of a father in the home prevents poor black youths from developing an adequate identification with work. Walter S. Neff, in *Work and Human Behavior* (Atherton, 1968), states: "A good case can be made that the male child of the very poor faces considerable difficulty in acquiring the components of the positive work personality. . . . If he is a child in a fatherless family, being brought up by his mother and an array of female relatives, then he will have difficulty imagining the role of the male breadwinner" (p. 248). It may well be true that the social manners and skills needed to obtain employment in middle-class occupations are not being transmitted to sons by poor mothers who are heads of families. This study makes it clear, however, that the sons in this situation are gaining a strong work ethic and that their mothers are probably playing a major role in the process.

8. Elizabeth Herzog and Cecelia E. Sudia, "Boys in Fatherless Families,"

U.S. Department of Health, Education, and Welfare, Office of Child Development, Children's Bureau (1970; processed).

CHAPTER 5

1. Ten teen-age WIN males (who have no children) have been removed from the group. The geographical distribution of the rest of the fathers correctly suggests that there are more men on the welfare rolls in the West than in the East. The respondents, however, cannot be said to be representative of all fathers receiving Aid to Families with Dependent Children (AFDC). They are probably typical of welfare fathers in nonsouthern cities who are judged fit to be enrolled in a work-training program. (Only about 5 percent of the more than 2 million adult AFDC recipients are fathers.)

CHAPTER 6

1. Table $_{C-6}$ shows that, if the groups making up the units in Table 6-1 were rearranged to form male and female units, males in general would be found to accept quasi-illegal activities more readily than females. This may reflect greater feminine rejection of such activities or merely the limited choice of activities listed under Orientation 4.

CHAPTER 7

1. In reviewing the records of each terminated WIN trainee, the author checked the reported length of time the trainee was in his job before termination. This was about twenty-six weeks in most cases.

2. The complete code for weekly earnings is as follows:

Code	Income (dollars)	Code	Income (dollars)
0	0	5	81–100
1	1–20	6	101–150
2	21–40	7	151–200
3	41–60	8	201–300
4	61–80	9	Over 300

3. The ratio of those employed to all those terminated is 214/551, or 0.39. This is considerably higher than the ratio of 0.20 for all WIN sites as reported in national data. The higher job rate in this study is accounted for by the exceptionally high rate in the District of Columbia WIN program.

See U.S. Department of Labor, Manpower Administration, "The Work Incentive Program: First Annual Report of the Department of Labor to the Congress on Training and Employment Under Title IV of the Social Security Act" (June 1970), p. 23.

4. The mean values given to acceptability of welfare by 302 welfare sons who are still in school are:

Grade completed	Age				
	15	16	17	18–19	No data
7	2.69	...	...	...	...
8	2.65	2.55	...	...	...
9	2.41	2.31	2.21	...	...
10	...	2.60	2.53	2.03	...
11	...	...	2.34	2.10	...
Number of sons	78	86	73	52	13

The pattern of means suggests that this orientation decreases with age even within the same grade level, as summarized in the correlation of -0.29 between age and the orientation. When educational level is controlled, the partial correlation is still a significant -0.16.

There are two possible explanations for these findings. The first is that increasing age, as such, reduces one's readiness to accept government support. This seems improbable because older students who are far behind their grade level (for example, nineteen-year-old students in the eleventh grade) might be expected to express more rather than less dependence on welfare. The second is that students with high ratings on the acceptability of welfare orientation begin to drop out of school in fairly large numbers when they reach sixteen and are no longer legally required to attend. The mean value of the ratings given Orientation 5 by students still in school, especially older students, would decrease because those with the highest ratings would have already dropped out. Indirectly, this reasoning leads to the inference that strong dependence on welfare both precedes and contributes to early termination of school by the poor.

5. Hubert M. Blalock, Jr., "Theory Building and Causal Inferences," in Hubert M. Blalock, Jr., and Ann B. Blalock (eds.), *Methodology in Social Research* (McGraw-Hill, 1968), pp. 155–98. A more rigorous approach to the analysis of causal sequences than looking at simple or partial correlations among variables is "path analysis." Because of the tentative nature of the causal sequences in this chapter, however, it seemed wiser to use the simpler approach. For a discussion of path analysis in relation to problems of causally ordering motivational variables, see Otis Dudley Duncan, "Con-

tingencies in Constructing Causal Models," in Edgar F. Borgatta (ed.), *Sociological Methodology 1969* (San Francisco: Jossey-Bass, 1969), pp. 74–112.

6. While differences in ratings at entrance to WIN and at reinterview are not as great as 0.33, which is the level established for judging significance of differences between means, the general pattern of these differences in relation to the causal sequence—high for orientations close to work activity in the sequence and low for the others—and the differences in ratings exhibited by the unemployed and employed groups argue for the validity of the findings.

7. For a more detailed examination of the work orientations and activities of WIN trainees, and the policy inferences to be drawn from the data, see Leonard Goodwin, "A Study of the Work Orientations of Welfare Recipients Participating in the Work Incentive Program," Final Report Submitted to the Office of Research and Development, Manpower Administration, U.S. Department of Labor (Brookings Institution, 1971; processed).

8. James S. Coleman and others, *Equality of Educational Opportunity*, U.S. Department of Health, Education, and Welfare (1966), pp. 24, 320–23.

9. Ibid., p. 21.

10. Arthur Jensen, "How Much Can We Boost IQ and Scholastic Achievement," *Harvard Educational Review*, Vol. 39 (Winter 1969), pp. 1–123. For comments on this article by J. M. Hunt, James Crow, Carl Bereiter, David Elkind, and Lee Cronbach, see *Harvard Educational Review*, Vol. 39 (Spring 1969), pp. 278–347.

11. Ray C. Rist, "Student Social Class and Teacher Expectations: The Self-Fulfilling Prophecy in Ghetto Education," *Harvard Educational Review*, Vol. 40 (August 1970), pp. 411–51. See also Robert Coles, *Teachers and the Children of Poverty* (Washington: Potomac Institute, 1970); and Charles E. Silberman, *Crisis in the Classroom: The Remaking of American Education* (Random House, 1970), pp. 53–112.

12. About 7 percent of the 500 black fathers and 3 percent of the 175 white fathers were unemployed at the time of interview. Most of these were receiving retirement or disability pensions, though a few were receiving unemployment compensation. These few unemployed fathers have been omitted from the analysis.

While it may seem inconsistent to eliminate the unemployed outer-city fathers when this was not done for the WIN women or the out-of-school welfare sons, who instead were given scores of zero, the unemployed fathers had been regular participants in the work force for a number of years, and their lack of employment is atypical of the group as a whole.

13. National data show, for example, that the average income in 1968 for black men older than twenty-five with one to three years of high school was $5,078. The income for their white counterparts was $6,973. See *Current Population Reports: Consumer Income*, U.S. Bureau of the Census, Series P-60, No. 66 (Dec. 23, 1969), p. 97. This finding may be the result in part of blacks showing less achievement than whites at the same grade level, as reported in Chapter 7.

CHAPTER 8

1. U.S. Department of Health, Education, and Welfare, Social and Rehabilitation Service, National Center for Social Statistics, "Preliminary Report of Findings—1969 AFDC Study" (March 1970; processed), pp. 2–3. See also Perry Levinson, "How Employable Are AFDC Women?" *Welfare in Review*, Vol. 8 (July–August 1970), pp. 12–16.

2. Department of Health, Education, and Welfare, "Services to AFDC Families: First Annual Report of the Department of Health, Education, and Welfare to the Congress on Services to Families Receiving Aid to Families with Dependent Children Under Title IV of the Social Security Act" (July 1970; processed), Table 2.

3. U.S. Department of Labor, Manpower Administration, "The Work Incentive Program: First Annual Report of the Department of Labor to the Congress on Training and Employment Under Title IV of the Social Security Act" (June 1970), p. 22.

4. Department of Labor, Manpower Administration, "Work Incentive Program: Table 18—Cumulative Enrollments and Terminations and Current Enrollment by Region, State and Project as of 2/28/71" (unpublished data; March 31, 1971).

5. The following statement was made by Elliot L. Richardson, secretary of Health, Education, and Welfare: "We have suggested that [welfare] recipients take jobs paying down to $1.20 per hour rather than providing no employment because all jobs at $1.60 or more an hour have been filled. There are presently over 7,000,000 jobs in our economy at less than $1.60 per hour, and we feel that the experience and skills to be gained from working . . . justify this position." *Washington Post* (Dec. 14, 1970), p. A22.

6. New legislation, amendments to Title II of the Social Security Act, requires one-third of WIN expenditures to be for public service employment or on-the-job training. See *Congressional Record*, daily ed., Dec. 14, 1971, p. H12446.

7. Gilbert Y. Steiner, *The State of Welfare* (Brookings Institution, 1971), p. 338.

8. Joseph A. Pechman, "The Rich, the Poor, and the Taxes They Pay," *The Public Interest*, No. 17 (Fall 1969), pp. 21–43 (Brookings Reprint 168).

9. Christopher Green, *Negative Taxes and the Poverty Problem* (Brookings, 1967). "The question of incentives inevitably arises when discussion turns to a proposal for a guaranteed minimum income. Would guaranteeing a minimum income and taxing it away at high rates as before-allowance income rises reduce work effort?" (p. 113).

10. Harold W. Watts, "Adjusted and Extended Preliminary Results from the Urban Graduated Work Incentive Experiment" (Madison: Institute for Research on Poverty, University of Wisconsin, 1970; processed). In a section called "Conclusion," Watts says, "The main impression left after a review of these crude analyses is that the experimental treatment has induced no dramatic or remarkable responses on the part of the families. . . . No evidence has been found in the urban experiment to support the belief that negative-tax-type income maintenance programs will produce large disincentives and consequent reductions in earnings" (pp. 38, 40). The same conclusion is maintained in a subsequent analysis of the experiment; see Office of Economic Opportunity, "Further Preliminary Results of the New Jersey Graduated Work Incentive Experiment" (May 1971; processed), p. 25.

11. Peter M. Blau and Otis Dudley Duncan, *The American Occupational Structure* (Wiley, 1967), p. 405; Bradley R. Schiller, "Stratified Opportunities: The Essence of the 'Vicious Circle,'" *American Journal of Sociology*, Vol. 76 (November 1970), pp. 426–42; Robert H. Berls, "Higher Education Opportunity and Achievement in the United States," in *The Economics and Financing of Higher Education in the United States*, A Compendium of Papers Submitted to the Joint Economic Committee, 91 Cong. 1 sess. (1969), especially pp. 146, 172; and William H. Sewell, "Inequality of Opportunity for Higher Education," *American Sociological Review*, Vol. 36 (October 1971), pp. 793–809. Researchers such as Sewell who present statistical data showing that poor children of the same ability as middle-class children do not reach the same educational attainment tend to explain this on the grounds of psychological deficiency, the poor having lower aspirations. Researchers who have examined the daily classroom procedure point out that it is the student-teacher interactions themselves which tend to lessen the aspirations and initiatives of the lower-class student as compared with his middle-class counterpart; see Eleanor Burke Leacock, *Teaching and Learning in City Schools* (Basic Books, 1969), Chap. 6. Lower educational aspirations of poor children would not appear to be a psychological deficiency, but a normal response to an environment hostile to their high aspirations and initiatives.

Index

Ability to succeed. *See* Confidence, lack of; Success
Achievement-motivation theory, 6–7
Action: determinants of, 89; relation to beliefs, goals, intentions, 113. *See also* Work activity
Action model, 9–12, 89–111
AFDC. *See* Aid to Families with Dependent Children
Affluence, 16, 110. *See also* Work beyond need for money
Aid to Families with Dependent Children, 17–18, 32, 104, 114; increase of, 157*n*.4. *See also* Mothers, welfare; Sons, welfare; Welfare system
Aspirations. *See* Life aspirations
Attitude: defined, 10–12, 159–60*n*.27; as element of work orientations, 14–18; measuring, 13–26

Baltimore, Md., 18–20, 33, 53, 70; Department of Welfare, 18, 32
Beliefs: defined, 10–12; as elements of work orientations, 14–18; measuring, 13–26; relation to action, 113. *See also* Luck
Bias. *See* Response bias
Blacks, 82–88; acceptability of welfare, 85; earlier studies, 3–5; effects of inferior opportunity, 87; effects of segregation, 86; job discrimination, 18, 85, 87; lack of confidence, 85–88; respon-

dents described, 18–22. *See also* Daughters; Fathers; Hickory Hill youths; Mothers; Sons; WIN trainees
Boys. *See* Hickory Hill youths; Sons

Caste system. *See* Segregation
Class status. *See* Response bias; Status, socioeconomic
Confidence, lack of (work orientation 3): correlation with acceptability of welfare, 80, 87–88, 97, 101, 111; correlation with life aspirations, 101, 111; correlation with work ethic, 59–61, 85, 97–99, 101, 107, 110–11; defined, 15–16; earnings related to, 106, 117; and educational achievement, 85–86, 107–08; effect of failure, 101, 103; effect on work activity, 69, 106–11, 116–17; of fathers, 75–77, 80, 81, 116–17; of mothers, 40–43, 51, 106–07; parental influence on, 67, 69, 106–07, 115; of races, compared, 75–77, 85–86; of sons, 59–61, 69, 106–07
Culture of poverty thesis, 2, 52, 86–88; 157*nn*.5–7

Daughters: number, 22, 82; sample described, 19–20; work ethic, 84
Discrimination, racial, 18; and outer-city blacks, 49–50, 64, 81. *See also* Job discrimination; Segregation
District of Columbia, 4, 20–21

174